ON SHAKY GROUND

Project Sponsors

Missouri Center for the Book

Western Historical Manuscript Collection,
University of Missouri–Columbia

Consultant

Donald M. Lance

Special Thanks

Susanna Alexander

Dorothy Merrill

A. E. Schroeder

Paul Szopa, Academic Support Center,
University of Missouri–Columbia

Sharon Sanders, *Southeast Missourian*

David Stewart

Missouri Heritage Readers

General Editor,

REBECCA B. SCHROEDER

Each Missouri Heritage Reader explores a particular aspect of the state's rich cultural heritage. Focusing on people, places, historical events, and the details of daily life, these books illustrate the ways in which people from all parts of the world contributed to the development of the state and the region. The books incorporate documentary and oral history, folklore, and informal literature in a way that makes these resources accessible to all Missourians.

Intended primarily for adult new readers, these books will also be invaluable to readers of all ages interested in the cultural and social history of Missouri.

Books in the Series

Food in Missouri: A Cultural Stew,
by Madeline Matson

Jesse James and the Civil War in Missouri,
by Robert L. Dyer

*On Shaky Ground: The New Madrid
Earthquakes of 1811–1812,*
by Norma Hayes Bagnall

*Paris, Tightwad, and Peculiar:
Missouri Place Names,*
by Margot Ford McMillen

The Trail of Tears across Missouri,
by Joan Gilbert

ON SHAKY GROUND

The New Madrid Earthquakes of 1811–1812

Norma Hayes Bagnall

University of Missouri Press
Columbia and London

Library of Congress Cataloging-in-Publication Data

Bagnall, Norma.
   On shaky ground : the New Madrid earthquakes of 1811–1812 / Norma
Bagnall.
      p. cm. — (Missouri heritage readers)
   Includes bibliographical references and index.
   Summary: Describes the severe earthquake which changed the course
of the Mississippi River in several places, destroyed timberlands, drained
swamps, and formed lakes.
   ISBN 0-8262-1054-6 (alk. paper)
   1. Earthquakes—Missouri—New Madrid Region—Juvenile literature.
[1. Earthquakes—Missouri—New Madrid.]   I. Title. II. Series.
QE535.2.U6B34   1996
977.8'985—dc20   95-26608
                                                      CIP
                                                       AC

Designer: Kristie Lee
Typesetter: BOOKCOMP
Printer and binder: Thomson-Shore, Inc.
Typefaces: Giovanni Book and Helvetica Neue

to my mother,

Alice Sloas Hayes

1907 – 1968

CONTENTS

ACKNOWLEDGMENTS

I want to express my appreciation to the participants on this project who carefully read the book in manuscript form. Their helpful and insightful suggestions have made it more readable.

I would also like to thank Kathleen Rohr, Co-Director of the Writing Project at St. Joseph, and Julia Brooke, Director of Pass the Power, a literacy center in St. Joseph. They read this work in an early stage and offered suggestions that I used in the final writing.

Linda Dillman, Associate Director of the Center for Earthquake Studies at Southeast Missouri State University, graciously shared information about earthquakes generally and about those on the New Madrid fault line specifically.

Fae Sotham and others on the staff of the State Historical Society of Missouri were of great help in locating pictures for this book. Always gracious and patient, they also directed me to original source material that enriched my knowledge of the earthquakes and of early Missouri history.

Joni Adams, Managing Editor of the *Southeast Missourian*, generously gave permission for the use of photographs. Sharon K. Sanders, a librarian with the *Southeast Missourian*, helped locate appropriate photos to use in this book. I appreciate their help.

In New Madrid, people were friendly and helpful while I was there gathering information. I want to especially thank William Clark, cafe owner; Martha Hunter, town librarian; and Clement Cravens, coeditor of the *New Madrid Weekly Gazette*. When they discovered I had come "back home" to research this book, they did everything they could to help me. They were generous in sharing their time, their resources, and their ideas.

Dr. David Stewart, former director of the Central United States Earthquake Center, kindly read my manuscript in its entirety. He has become a friend during my work on this manuscript, as he offered suggestions, praise, and a wealth of information about geological phenomena. I am grateful for his careful and thorough reading and for his professional advice.

My colleagues at Missouri Western State College supported my request for a sabbatical leave, and I thank them for their interest in my work and for taking on the duties that otherwise would have been mine in spring 1994. I also want to thank the administrators at Missouri Western, who have encouraged me in my work and supported my request for leave. Finally, I want to thank the Board of Regents at the college; they generously granted the request for the sabbatical leave that allowed me the time and energy to complete this book.

ON SHAKY GROUND

New Madrid is located on the northern edge of the "Bootheel" section of Missouri, in the southeastern corner of the state. It lies on the Mississippi River and is much closer to some cities in Tennessee, Kentucky, and Arkansas than to St. Louis. The town is on an oxbow bend in the river, north of the river near the center of the upside-down U. Across the river to the south, the Kentucky bank is clearly visible. But this part of Kentucky is cut off from the rest of its state by the unusual bend in the river.

From the observation deck at New Madrid, looking southeast to island and Kentucky. (photo by the author)

My mother grew up in Marston and New Madrid, Missouri, in the early part of the twentieth century. Stories about the earthquakes of 1811–1812 were part of her childhood. They also became part of my own childhood as she retold the stories to my sister and me.

Mother listened, big-eyed, to stories that the Mississippi River ran backward for three days. She heard that people had to cut down large trees across the cracks made in the earth's surface and hold on to them to keep from being swallowed during the quakes. She could see for herself islands in the river that had been created by the quakes; she learned that other islands had disappeared. She could still see evidence of forests that had tumbled into the river when its banks caved in. Tree trunks still poked up out of the water at the river's edge. She learned that if she had been born a century earlier, her birthplace would be about halfway across the Mississippi River. That was where New Madrid had been located before the ground sank after the quakes.

As a girl, Mother walked barefoot in the mud on the shores of the Mississippi with her sister and her friends. She could see evidence of the changes the quakes had left on the landscape in Marston and New Madrid as water had covered the area. The remains of sinkholes were still visible, and where the town of New Madrid had once been, there was only water.

When Mother moved to St. Louis as a teenager in the 1920s, she searched out the "St. Louis Hills" section on the city's south side. She had been told that the "Hills" were formed during the New Madrid earthquake. As a child, I also heard, from my mother and from others, that the "St. Louis Hills" are a result of the quakes. I have learned since that they probably are not. I have never seen any evidence that the earthquakes caused any changes in the St. Louis landscape.

All the evidence we have indicates that the quakes we call the "New Madrid earthquake" were indeed "the big one." Most often, we use the word *earthquake* to describe the events of 1811–1812, as if there had been only one quake, but there were actually

Alice Sloas Hayes and Pasha Sloas, mother and aunt of the author, about 1926. There is a saying that "once the Mississippi mud gets between your toes, you never stray far from the river."

repeated quakes over several months. Some scientists believe that all the shakings were the result of one massive quake and its aftershocks. Some of the aftershocks were very severe; one was even stronger than the first quakes.

The Richter scale that measures the size or magnitude of earthquakes and the Mercalli scale that measures the intensity of quakes were not developed until the twentieth century. Eyewitness accounts, earth changes, and the vast area affected, however, show that these quakes were larger than any other ever reported on the North American continent. They are also unique because they lasted longer than any other set of earthquakes in North America. During the months of the most severe quakes, December 1811 to February 1812, the earth on the New Madrid fault line was constantly in turmoil.

In an article in the *Kansas City Star* on May 5, 1987, Isaac Asimov wrote, "The most severe earthquake in the history of the United States took place Feb. 7, 1812, not in California, but on the Mississippi River near New Madrid. . . . It destroyed 150,000 acres of timberland, changed the course of the Mississippi in several places, drained . . . swamps and formed . . . lakes."

On a day-to-day basis the people of New Madrid pay little or no attention to the fact that they live on a major fault line. They are far more concerned with the cost of fertilizer, the price of corn, cotton, and soybeans, and whether or not rains will come (or stop) in time to save the crops.

But for the people then living in New Madrid, the winter of 1811–1812 was a different story.

CHAPTER 1

Early History of New Madrid

"In 1799, New Madrid was the gateway for all trade between the Allegheny Mountains and the Gulf of Mexico by way of the Mississippi River."

—Earl A. Collins and Felix Eugene Snider, *Missouri: Midland State*

The Earliest Americans

Indians had lived in the area that is now southeast Missouri for thousands of years before European settlers began coming to the area. It was a good place to hunt. Black bear, elk, cougar, bison, and antelope lived there in great abundance in the late 1600s.

The New Madrid area was first called by the French name *L'Anse à la Graisse*, which means "cove of fat" or "cove of grease," because there was so much game there, especially bear. French hunters and trappers sold or traded bear meat and other meats to passing boat crews. Indians also traded there. In the winter, they had deerskins and bearskins as well as smaller animal skins to barter. In the summer, they traded honey and bear oil.

The Indians living in southeast Missouri during early settlement by the French and Americans were primarily from the Delaware and Shawnee tribes. To the north, Kaskaskia Indians

Kishkahna, Shawnee chief. Bands of Shawnee Indians began to settle west of the Mississippi River in about 1780. (State Historical Society of Missouri, Columbia)

lived at the mouth of the River Des Peres, now a part of St. Louis. The Kaskaskias had left their village in Illinois to escape crowding and attacks as other tribes moved into what had been their territory. There may also have been Quapaw Indians in southeast Missouri.

Teciekeapease, the sister of Tecumseh, the great Shawnee chief, was a member of a tribe who moved west of the Mississippi River and settled in what is now Uniontown, north of Cape Girardeau, in Perry County, Missouri. Teciekeapease was noted for her beauty and intelligence. When she traveled to New Madrid to visit some of her tribe living in the area, she fell in love with a French Creole, François Maisonville, and married him in 1808. This marriage angered Tecumseh, who forced her to return to her own settlement. However, she stayed only a few months with her people and then went back to her husband in New Madrid, where she was during the earthquakes. Her long and happy marriage produced twelve children.

Teciekeapese, sister of the Shawnee leader Tecumseh, who did not approve of her marriage to a Frenchman. He took her back to her own people, but she returned to her husband when Tecumseh left. She lived in the New Madrid area at the time of the quakes. (State Historical Society of Missouri, Columbia)

Tecumseh. The Shawnee leader, born in Ohio in about 1768, was admired as a great warrior who showed compassion for enemies. He dreamed of unifying Indian tribes to stop white settlers from pushing farther west. He would not allow a portrait to be made of him by white people, and this likeness is based on a pencil sketch made in 1810 by a French trader, Pierre Le Dru, in Vincennes in the Indiana Territory and a sketch later found in Montreal, Canada, published in Benson J. Loessing's *The Pictorial Field-Book of the War of 1812*. (State Historical Society of Missouri, Columbia)

Indians were being forced out of lands east of the Mississippi River because of the advance of American settlers. The power, guns, and sheer numbers of the new settlers overwhelmed the Indians, and they had little choice but to move or be moved west. The American government protected American pioneers and their interests and showed little or no sympathy for Indian land claims. The anger the Indians felt frequently resulted in raids on the new settlements on both sides of the Mississippi River.

Spanish Exploration

North America west of the Mississippi River was almost unknown to Europeans until the late 1600s. Spanish treasure hunters had searched there for valuable minerals, and some

Hernando de Soto, a sixteenth-century Spanish explorer. De Soto reached the lower Mississippi River in 1541. Some historians believe that de Soto traveled up the west side of the river to southeast Missouri. (State Historical Society of Missouri, Columbia)

believe that explorer Francisco Coronado and his men may have ventured northeast from Mexico into Missouri to search for gold during the sixteenth century. If this is true, the explorers did not remain long, probably because Missouri did not offer them the riches they wanted.

In 1541, according to legend, during the time of a great drought, the Spanish explorer Hernando de Soto visited what is now part of the New Madrid area. He so charmed the Indians that they asked him to pray to his god for rain.

One historian reports that de Soto ordered his men to build a large cross of cypress and raise it on a mound of earth near the river. He and his men, joined by the Indians, celebrated Catholic Mass there, close to the site where New Madrid was built more than 200 years later. This means that the first Christian worship on the west side of the Mississippi River may have been held in Missouri. We do not know whether rain came and saved the crops.

Historian William Parrish believes that de Soto arrived in Arkansas opposite what is now Memphis, Tennessee, in 1541. He heard from Indians near his camp that salt and a yellow metal could be found to the north. De Soto, who was exploring to find gold and riches, probably would have gone north to find the treasure when he heard this. Parrish suggests that de Soto and his men may have traveled as far north as the Saline River near Ste. Genevieve, Missouri.

Traveling in 1540 from their base in Florida, de Soto's party crossed the Mississippi River and explored the area around present-day Helena, Arkansas. Don Kurz, writing in the *Missouri Conservationist* in July 1991, suggested that de Soto followed Crowley's Ridge north from what is now Arkansas to what is now Missouri and was the first European explorer in that area. De Soto then moved northward along the ridge to a point somewhere in what is now Dunklin County. He likely followed Indian trails. Of the numerous Indian paths and trails on Crowley's Ridge, the Shawnee Trail was the best known and most widely used.

Historian William Foley thinks that de Soto did not get to Missouri. Foley also believes that Coronado in his explorations did not venture farther east than Kansas and so never came to Missouri. The Mississippi Valley area in southeastern Missouri was not of much interest to early Spanish explorers. They were interested in mining gold and silver, not in building colonies for settlers. It was left to later pioneers to begin the European-American settlement of the land that became Missouri.

French Settlement

In June 1673, a young French trader and explorer, Louis Jolliet, was sent by French officials from Quebec to St. Ignace, Michigan, and joined a Jesuit priest, Jacques Marquette, on an exploration of the Mississippi River. Foley believes that Jolliet and Marquette were the first Europeans to set foot in Missouri.

Jolliet and Marquette wanted to learn more about the Mississippi River. At that time, explorers did not know the location of the mouth of the Mississippi. Some guessed that the river might flow east toward Virginia; others believed it turned west to the Pacific Ocean. By the time Jolliet and Marquette reached Arkansas, they knew that the river was headed for the Gulf of Mexico. It was not until nine years later, in 1682, that Robert Cavelier, sieur de La Salle, another Frenchman, followed the river to its mouth. He claimed the entire area for France.

More French people came in the late seventeenth century to settle their lands along the Mississippi River. They were the first to challenge Spain's hold on all lands west of the Mississippi. Both England and France wanted to expand their lands in America at this time. While the English settled mostly on the eastern seaboard of the "New World," the French were interested in the St. Lawrence waterways. They established Quebec in 1608, and in 1673 they began exploration of the Mississippi River valley. In 1682, when La Salle claimed the Mississippi and the land west of it for the French, the territory west of the river was named Louisiana in honor of King Louis XIV.

Tish-Co-Han, Delaware chief. Delaware Indians began to cross the Mississippi and settle in Spanish Territory around 1780. (State Historical Society of Missouri, Columbia)

In 1762, near the end of a war between the French and the English, King Louis XV of France decided to cede the Louisiana Territory to his cousin, King Charles III, of Spain. As Foley states, with the stroke of a pen the territory switched from French to Spanish rule. Life for the French settlers did not change much under the Spanish. The area was sometimes called Upper Louisiana, sometimes New Spain, showing the territory's ties with both France and Spain. It remained under Spanish rule until it was traded back to France in 1800, when Napoleon ruled France. The French leader feared that the British or Americans might capture the small Spanish garrisons at New Madrid and St. Louis and lay claim to New Spain.

In the 1780s Jean Gabriel Cerré, who had moved to St. Louis to develop a fur-trading business, sent François LeSieur and his brother Joseph, French-Canadian fur trappers, down the river to find a place closer to New Orleans where a trading post could be established. They settled near a large Delaware Indian village and set up a post. They intended to trade with the Indians and build up a profitable business. Their trading post is considered the first permanent European settlement in what was later to be New Madrid. The area kept the name "Cove of Grease" that it was called when only Indian traders lived there. The LeSieurs remained in the area, and the third child of François LeSieur, Godfrey, was an area businessman during the earthquakes of 1811–1812.

The rich Mississippi River bottomlands produced generous crops. The river provided a natural means for trappers and farmers to trade their furs and other goods for those things the area did not provide. Although the area gained some population during Spanish and French rule, it remained remote and sparsely populated. Roads were poorly marked trails, and newcomers needed a trained guide to find their way through them.

George Morgan

In 1789, Colonel George Morgan of New Jersey, traveling with seventy men in four large boats, arrived in southeastern Missouri looking for new lands to settle. Diego de Gardoqui, the Spanish minister to the United States, was trying to promote settlement on Spanish land west of the Mississippi River. He had promised Morgan twelve million acres of land if he could establish a colony. Morgan was a patriot of the American Revolution. He had also been an Indian agent, a public official, a trader, and a land speculator. He now wanted to buy land, build a town, and sell lots to new settlers. Morgan expected the new town to bring him both wealth and importance. He had been disappointed trying to deal with the government of the newly independent United States, so Gardoqui's scheme appealed to him. Morgan chose what would be the New Madrid area to build his planned city.

Morgan had earlier tried to settle areas east of the Mississippi, first in Indiana and then in Illinois. He had lost money on some of his earlier ventures and was frustrated with barriers

George Morgan. Morgan had served as an officer in the American Revolutionary War and as a U.S. Indian agent. He planned the town of New Madrid in 1789. (copyright Washington County Historical Society, Washington, Pa.)

the United States government put in the way of his success. Moving across the Mississippi River put him under Spanish rule, but he saw no problem with that. New Madrid was the place where he thought he could create a thriving town and become rich. The site was already established as a good place for fur traders.

Handbills were distributed across the eastern part of the United States to lure people to the "Western Lands," as the area west of the Mississippi River was called. Each man who came to the settlement would be able to buy up to 320 acres of land at 12½ cents per acre. He was promised free navigation of the Mississippi River, which was a major attraction. Corn raised on a "common ground" would be available the first season (after the first settlers had raised it) at 12½ cents per bushel. Morgan assumed that families would build their own cabins and begin working their own land during the first year. Then they could live independently on their own property. The common ground would be used by new settlers as they arrived. Wild game was available to hunters; those unlucky in the hunt could buy venison or beef at 1 cent per pound.

Morgan had recognized the importance of the New Madrid location. It was on the Mississippi River but was protected from the river by high ground. The Ohio River, which was used to ship goods to the East, was only 70 miles by river to the north. The Osage River, 150 miles inland from the Mississippi River, was important to Morgan's plan. He wanted New Madrid to take over the fur trade that had been going by way of the Osage River to St. Louis for shipment to New Orleans. He believed that, as a shipping port, New Madrid was more accessible to the trappers than St. Louis was.

The Osage River joins the Missouri River east of what is now Jefferson City, and trade had been going from the Osage River east on the Missouri River, winding its way about 125 miles to St. Louis, which is over 250 miles north of New Madrid by river. A trip from New Madrid to New Orleans, which had a large market for furs and other goods, could be made in about 20 days by way of the Mississippi River. Morgan saw New Madrid becoming a major trading center that could be linked to all the world's markets because of its favorable location.

A letter written in New Madrid on April 14, 1788, to promote the settlement was published in the *Virginia Gazette and Weekly Advertiser* on August 27 of that year. It described the site of the city: "Here the banks of the Mississippi . . . are high, dry and pleasant, and the land westward to the river St. Francois is [suitable] for Indian corn, tobacco, flax, cotton, hemp and indigo." Some thought the land to be too rich for wheat. The land was higher than the area around it, and explorers believed that it would be safe from flooding. (Arch Johnston, director of the Center for Earthquake Research and Information at Memphis State University, comments that no one seemed to worry about why this land was raised above the surrounding area.)

Morgan outlined in detail the kind of town he wanted to establish. It was to be "four miles long and two miles wide." There were to be 10 broad streets parallel to the river, each 60 feet wide, and 18 streets running back from the river, each 45 feet wide. Six public squares were planned, and land was to be set aside for schools and churches. One-half-acre lots in the city and five-acre parcels outside of town were offered to the first 600 settlers. Half a section of land (320 acres) was set aside for each of 350 families. On the waterfront, Morgan planned a street 120 feet wide; there he wanted to build government buildings and a fort. He also planned a convenient marketplace and a central storehouse.

The letter in the *Virginia Gazette and Weekly Advertiser* gave further details on the planned city:

> The limits of the new city of Madrid are to extend four miles south and down the river, and two miles west from it, so as to cross a beautiful deep lake, of the purest spring water, 100 yards wide . . . emptying itself by a constant narrow stream through the center of the city.

Morgan knew of the importance of the natural environment to the welfare of a new town. In his concern for preserving the environment, he was well ahead of his time. He planned to be chief magistrate, and he made rules that would ban the cutting down of trees and shrubs without his permission. He also showed concern for Indians and for wildlife. Professional white hunters would not be allowed to live within the town. Morgan would allow settlers to kill only the buffalo and deer they needed to feed themselves and their families, because he knew the Indians in the area depended on hunting to make a living. Morgan had invited Indians representing several tribes to come down the Ohio River with him. He wanted them to see what he was doing so they could learn to trust him. The letter also affirmed Morgan's intention to respect Indian lands: "There is not a single nation or tribe of Indians who claims or pretends to claim, a foot of land granted to Colonel Morgan."

Morgan wanted his town to be the capital of the Spanish empire in America. The Mississippi River had been closed to

Americans and was now open only to those who paid taxes to the Spanish government at New Orleans. Kentuckians and other American settlers on the east side of the river were angry at Spain's control over the Mississippi, but they had few options; they needed the river for trade. Morgan did not intend to change the system. He believed that keeping the tariffs would strengthen New Madrid and bring moneys to himself. Gardoqui, the Spanish minister, had assured him of the cooperation of the Spanish government at New Orleans.

In the summer of 1789, Morgan traveled to New Orleans to talk about his town with Don Estevan Miró, governor of Louisiana and ruler of the Spanish territory to the north. He knew that Governor Miró did not like "Cove of Fat" as a town name, and Morgan also wanted a more impressive name for his town. He decided to call the town New Madrid, hoping to please the Spanish by honoring Spain's capital city. (In Spain, *Madrid* is pronounced with stress on the second syllable, "muh-DRID." In Missouri, we pronounce it "MAA-drid," with stress on the first syllable.)

Miró was not pleased with the idea of Morgan's being in charge of a Spanish town and fort. He had been influenced by James A. Wilkinson, an early wheeler-dealer who had suggested that Miró entice Kentuckians to settle west of the Mississippi River with the offer of free lands. Spain's policy until the 1770s had been to restrict lands west of the river to Spanish Catholics. By 1787, though, the Spanish were offering lands to American Protestants and promising religious tolerance. But Wilkinson wanted to restrict American settlements west of the river in order to gain prominence and wealth for himself. Apparently he persuaded Miró that an agreement with Morgan would be harmful to Spain's interest.

Miró had been offering free land to attract new settlers, and he refused to agree to Morgan's plan to sell land in Spanish Louisiana. He also did not want to lose control by allowing Morgan to be commandant; he instead named a Spaniard as commandant, with Morgan second in command. Miró offered

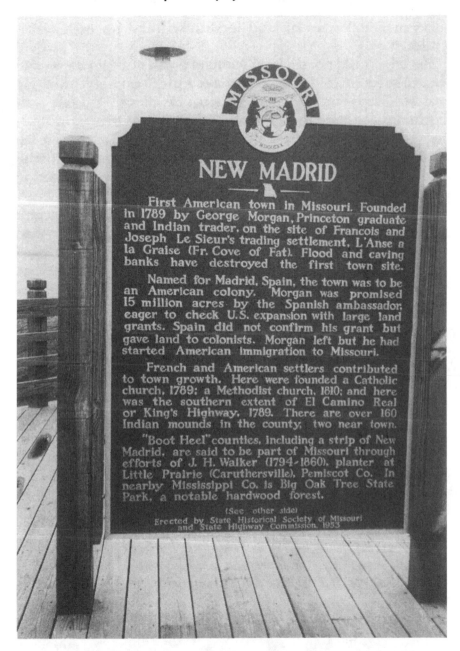

State marker erected in New Madrid in 1953 by the State Historical Society of Missouri and the State Highway Commission. (photo by the author)

Morgan 1,000 acres of land for himself and for each of his children.

But if he could not *sell* land, Morgan could not gain the wealth he expected; he could not even make a profit on his venture. He was so disappointed that he gave up his plans. Without even bothering to return to New Madrid from New Orleans, Morgan moved back to New Jersey and then to Pennsylvania, where his brother had left him a large estate. Of the seventy men who had come to New Madrid with him, only fourteen decided to stay.

However, Morgan's circulars, which had already been sent around the eastern states to promote the new city, attracted another wave of settlers. They came and built cabins and fenced garden spots on their half-acres of ground; they also helped build the storehouse and prepare the common field. The first school was erected and operating by 1793. Farming was a good reason for settling in New Madrid, and the fur trade was also important. The river, however, was the main reason; it had created a fertile land and provided a handy way for the new settlers to trade their goods.

For the town he had named, the years following Morgan's arrival in 1789 were peaceful and prosperous. In 1796–1797 an Englishman, Francis Baily, toured the Ohio and Mississippi valleys and described New Madrid:

> New Madrid is situated on a level plain which extends a considerable way into the country, on the western bank of the Mississippi, just opposite an island which stands nearly in the middle of the river. . . . two or three hundred houses [are] scattered about . . . within a mile or so of the fort. . . . (*Journal of a Tour in Unsettled Parts of North America in 1796–1797*)

Baily reported that the fort stood in the center of a square in the middle of town and contained "from thirty to forty men." He noted that while his boat was at New Madrid, Indians came to trade deerskins and bearskins and beaver furs: "These articles pass . . . as money."

New Madrid became the most important landing between the Ohio River and Natchez, Mississippi. New settlers built homes and schools. There were stores where goods could be bought and sold. New Protestant churches were built. Because the king of Spain had first allowed only members of the Catholic Church to settle west of the Mississippi River, many of the early settlers had been French pioneers, who were Catholic. There had been almost no American settlers before Morgan began the town, because most Americans were Protestants. The French had settled in town, with houses near the street and close together. The Americans usually settled out of town, where they had more space.

Life in New Madrid revolved around the river and the important trade it brought. A report that incorrectly located the town in Tennessee, "Notes of a Journey from Philadelphia to New Madrid, Tennessee 1790," published by the *Pennsylvania Magazine of History and Biography,* shows that "flour was exchanged for furs for the following prices per skin: Bear, $1, Wildcat, 65 cents, Otter, $3, Beaver, $1, Buffalo $10."

In his report in 1797, Francis Baily gave some prices in French coin, some in American dollars. Sheared deerskins were selling for 40 sous, or 2 livres, per pound; beaver, 120 sous, or 6 livres, per pound. Otter skins sold for $4 each, and raccoon for 25 cents. Baily wrote, "Skins at this price are legal tender in all payments."

In 1803, the town of New Madrid and the surrounding area were a part of the Louisiana Purchase, and thus became part of the United States. James Wilkinson, the first territorial governor, served from 1805 to 1807. Meriwether Lewis, the Lewis of the Lewis and Clark expedition, became the second governor of the territory in 1808. By then, New Madrid was a thriving town.

The people living in New Madrid were aware of the potential danger of the river. It overflowed its bounds now and then. But they had no idea that underneath the river and the land there was a huge rift in the earth's crust. The evidence was there, in the form of sand boils and swampy land, but only a scientist would have recognized the signs. The settlers had no way of knowing the edges of the rift could rub together and cause the most violent earthquakes that had ever happened within the recorded history of humans on the North American continent.

CHAPTER 2

The First Quakes

"No pencil can paint the distress of many movers. Men, women, and children, barefooted and naked, without money and food."

— Newspaper account in *Some Happenings of the New Madrid Earthquake, 1811–1812*, compiled by Dorothy H. Halstead

On Sunday evening, December 15, 1811, there was no reason for the people in New Madrid to think that their lives would be changed by morning. Crops were in, and the gathering of fruits and vegetables had been finished long before. British-American settlers who were members of a Protestant church had probably spent most of the day in worship. In the early evening, there may have been visiting among neighbors. Many of New Madrid's early settlers were French, and after Sunday services they often had parties or dances. New Madrid had private schools, and children may have had homework to finish before morning. They would also have been thinking about Christmas, which was just ten days away.

The weather had been rainy in New Madrid that December. Both the Ohio and the Mississippi rivers had flooded in the spring, but that was not unusual. A comet with two tails had appeared in September; some people thought comets foretold bad luck to come. William Pierce, traveling on the Mississippi

River just south of New Madrid, reported that for three days prior to the first quakes the sky had been overcast and the weather "thick and heavy."

Thunderstorms had occurred later in the season than was usual, but the evening of December 15 in New Madrid was cold and clear. It was quiet as well. Farmers on the edge of town checked on their livestock, which were secure in sheds or behind fences. People got ready for bed; they may have put water near the fireplace to heat at morning's first light. They stoked their fires, blew out their lamps, and went to bed.

Just after 2 A.M. those who had gone to sleep were awakened by a loud noise. It sounded like "loud and distant thunder." The noise was followed at once by a movement of their houses. Logs shifted and creaked; dishes and jars fell from shelves and tables. Bricks from chimneys came loose and fell. People ran from their homes to escape the falling bricks and moving walls. According to eyewitness A. N. Dillard, the French people were still partying and dancing when the first quake hit.

The settlers stayed outdoors the rest of that cold December night. The tremors continued throughout the early morning hours, coming from eight to thirty minutes apart. The people were afraid to go back into their homes. Furniture was moving, walls were creaking, and houses continued to shift. It seemed safer to remain outdoors.

In the morning they had little time to see what harm had been done to their homes. At about 7 A.M. another large quake occurred, as strong or stronger than the first one. People could not see much because the air was filled with fog and vapors, but they could see that the earth was moving in billowy patterns, like the rolling of the sea or like fields of wheat moving in the wind. Depressions in the earth often burst and sent up sand, water, small rocks, and what seemed to be coal. The next large quake occurred near 11 A.M. Scientists believe this quake was the strongest of the three. The fog and vapors from the cracks in the earth stayed in the area for more than a full day after the first quakes. People complained about the terrible smell, saying it was like sulfur.

"Family in terror on doorstep" during the earthquake. Eyewitnesses described the horror of the night of the first earthquake: A "noise like thunder" came before the first violent quake. "Then the air was saturated with sulphurous vapor and the night made loud with the cries of fowls and animals, the cracking of the trees, and the surging torrent of the Mississippi," which came rushing down in thirty-foot waves. People were afraid to go back into their homes, so they stayed outside for the rest of the night. (State Historical Society of Missouri, Columbia)

These three large quakes were the beginning of what would become known as the New Madrid earthquake. Scientists agree that the center of the first of the three quakes was near the Arkansas-Missouri border, about sixty miles south and a bit west of New Madrid. No record exists of settlers in that area, but probably fur trappers, Indians, and some early settlers lived there. Blytheville, Arkansas, is now located very near that first center. The second quake centered just south of what is now Steele, Missouri. The 11 A.M. quake's center was at Little Prairie, now Caruthersville, Missouri.

There would be more. Tremors continued to rock the area for weeks, and on January 23, 1812, there was another quake centered about ten miles north of Little Prairie, closer to New Madrid. The biggest quake hit just south of Marston, Missouri, about seven miles south of New Madrid. On that spot on present-day Interstate Highway 55 there is now a "Welcome to Missouri" information center. The quakes followed a line generally north and slightly east, coming nearer and nearer to New Madrid.

Little Prairie

Ben Chartier was sixteen at the time of the first quake. He lived in Little Prairie, thirty miles closer to the quake's center than New Madrid. He was interviewed seventy years later (in 1881) for the *Weekly Record,* New Madrid's newspaper, and gave his account of the first "shake," as he called it. He remembered that when the first moving of the earth came, his father turned the hogs out. The ground burst open, taking down fruit trees. Then the earth spewed up sand and water and forced the trees back up.

The Chartier family ran toward New Madrid through the woods. Jake LeSier, a young black man, carried Ben's younger brother. Chartier said that Jake fell and the little boy's nose was smashed. Chartier also remembered that the "earth broke open and trees fell across, so we had to coon the logs." He meant that they went astride them, as he thought raccoons would. He also reported that he and his family covered the distance from Little Prairie to New Madrid (more than twenty-five miles) in one day.

Chartier's memory at age eighty-six could have been faulty. The event he remembered not only was frightening at the time, but also had occurred so many years before the interview. However, even if his facts are not accurate, the sense of the fear he and his family felt remained vivid in his mind. In Chartier's memory, there were no stores in New Madrid at the time of the earthquakes. People made all of their clothes, Chartier said, including shoes. They made their hats out of coon, fox, or possum furs and their shoes out of wood or rawhide. However, we know that Robert Watson was a licensed merchant in New Madrid and that he had been there since 1804; there were two other licensed merchants as well. Since he lived in Little Prairie, Ben Chartier may not have known about the stores in New Madrid.

David Stewart, a geoscientist, founded and directed the Center for Earthquake Studies at Cape Girardeau from 1989 to 1991. He and Ray Knox developed a different account of the events that took place the night of December 15–16. They believe that Little Prairie was flooded by the quake and the settlers there had to walk through eight miles of waist-high water to get to higher ground. People did not know whether they were going to sink into water over their heads or trip over a submerged stump with each step they took. They also had to contend with snakes and other wild animals swimming for their lives. They did not know if they would live until the end of the day. But all survived.

The next day, Stewart and Knox say, they began to make their way to New Madrid. They had no idea that the earthquakes had affected anyone besides themselves. It was a hard journey because the quakes had made what had been a fairly clear trail into a mass of tangled trees and branches. Much of the once-dry trail was covered with muddy water. Crevasses and quicksand, also caused by the quakes, added to the dangers of the trip. They

"The banks above, below and around us were falling every moment into the river, all nature seemed running into chaos." John Bradbury, a British scientist, was on a keelboat on the Mississippi about a hundred miles south of New Madrid in the early morning of December 16, 1811, and described the noise of the earthquake itself, the screaming of the birds, and the sound of the high banks falling into the river. Many boat crews and passengers were lost during the earthquake. ("Scene of the Great Earthquake in the West," from *Our First Century*, published in 1877. State Historical Society of Missouri, Columbia)

also had to contend with the darkness and a smell of sulfur that came from the quakes. Little Prairie refugees arrived in New Madrid eight days after the first quakes, on Christmas Eve, but the town was deserted. The settlers there had moved out of their broken and ruined houses and were camped about two miles northwest of town.

William Atkinson, the author of *The Next New Madrid Earthquake*, believes that the first quake at 2 A.M. on December 16 caused equal amounts of damage in New Madrid and in Little Prairie, both on the Mississippi River. However, the 7 A.M. quake on December 16 destroyed almost every home in Little Prairie.

The entire riverbank there fell into the river and was carried away by the raging stream. Some of the settlers left the town in the middle of the night after the first quake. It must have been "a scene of horror in those deep forests and in the gloom of the darkest night," as Timothy Flint wrote. Flint, a Presbyterian minister, was in the area less than ten years later. Little Prairie settlers who had stayed through the night left quickly after the 7 A.M. quake because the river was claiming the town. Before the end of December, the town of Little Prairie was gone; everything was under water.

The Richter scale for measuring the size or magnitude of earthquakes would not be developed until 1935, but from the extensive damage and reports of eyewitnesses, scientists today believe that the quakes on the morning of December 16 would have measured 8.0 or more on that scale. An earthquake measuring as low as 5.0 on the Richter scale can do major damage near the epicenter, which is the spot on the earth's surface directly above the source of the quake.

At the time the quakes hit, New Madrid was a busy market town, but it had a population of only about 800 to 1,000. There were probably 100 or so settlers in Little Prairie. Farmers, hunters, and trappers lived outside these villages, but there is no exact record of how many there were. The river during the quakes was in constant turmoil, claiming riverbanks and throwing up trees and other debris that had been under the surface. There were boat crews lost on the river, but there was no reliable way of counting people, so many deaths went unreported. It is assumed that most deaths resulting from the New Madrid earthquakes were caused by drowning.

Stewart and Knox report ten deaths caused by the December 16 quakes. Six Indians drowned when the riverbanks caved in and threw them into the Mississippi River. A woman refused to leave her cabin and was killed by falling debris; another woman panicked and ran until she suffered a massive heart attack. One man was drowned when he fell into a sand-blow crater that appeared during the quake that was filled with quicksand;

another man, ill to begin with, did not survive the shock brought on by camping out following the early quakes in mid-December.

Most of the buildings in the quake area were of frame or log; both are much more resistant to the earth's movement than are stone, brick, or concrete. The buildings were also only one story high. Multistory buildings are in much more danger of collapsing during earthquakes. But when the New Madrid quakes were over, most of the buildings in the area had been damaged or destroyed.

Eyewitness Reports

One of the most thorough descriptions of the horror that people felt during the quakes is the letter written in 1816 by Eliza Bryan, a schoolteacher who lived near New Madrid at the time of the quakes with her parents, sisters, and brothers. A Methodist minister, Lorenzo Dow, asked Bryan to write about the earthquakes as she remembered them. He included her letter in the journal he published. Bryan served as a model for a character in Henry Kroll's novel *Fury in the Earth*, set in New Madrid during the quakes. Her descriptions of the quakes provide background for the novel.

Eliza Bryan's writing is clear and detailed. Her account, written four years after the last quakes, is chronological. Bryan recalled that the morning of the first quake, "we were visited by a violent shock of an earthquake, accompanied by a very awful noise, resembling loud but distant thunder, but more hoarse and vibrating." She added that in "all of the hard shocks the earth was horribly torn to pieces; the surface of hundreds of acres was from time to time covered over of various depths by the sand which issued from the fissures."

Within a few minutes, Bryan wrote, the air became filled with a vapor that smelled like sulfur. People were running back and forth and did not know where to go or what to do. Nights are dark when there is only the light of the moon and stars, and that was the case in New Madrid at that time period. On the

The New Madrid earthquake was "the big one." Colonel John Shaw was in New Madrid on the morning of February 7, 1812, when "nearly two thousand people of all ages, fled in terror from their falling dwellings" in New Madrid itself and the surrounding country. ("The Great Earthquake in New Madrid," from Henry Howe's *The Great West*, published in Cincinnati in 1851. State Historical Society of Missouri, Columbia)

frontier, there were no streetlights, auto lights, or neon signs to lighten the darkness. After the quakes, the night became darker because of fog and vapors that spewed from the earth. Bryan reported that there was almost total darkness the morning of December 16.

She told of the sound of animals bleating and bawling. Chickens and other birds were screeching and squawking. People could hear trees cracking and falling. Nearby, the Mississippi River roared without stop. The roaring water claimed riverbanks and forests of trees that tumbled into it. The quakes continued throughout the night, but they became weaker as morning neared. The noises, smells, and panic continued as well, through the quakes that occurred at about 7 A.M. and 11 A.M. Then there was a settling.

John Bradbury, a well-known British botanist, was also in the quake area. He was traveling down the Mississippi on a keelboat loaded with lead bound for New Orleans. Bradbury had already sent his collection of American plant specimens to the Gulf city. He claimed that after the shock occurred, the steep banks of the river "both above and below us, began to fall into the river in such vast masses, as nearly to sink our boat by the swell they [caused]."

Later Quakes

Minor quakes continued for over a month, but then on January 23, there was another severe one. Louis Bringier, an engineer and land surveyor, was in the New Madrid area in January 1812 and reported that the quakes had forced water up from the earth in roaring explosions carrying with it carbonized wood dust and sand in spouts ten to fifteen feet high. Bringier wrote that "the roaring and whistling of the air escaping [from the earth], seemed to increase the horrible disorder of the trees [which were] blown up, cracking and splitting and falling by thousands at a time." The surface of the land was sinking, he wrote, and a black liquid, which was probably a mixture of carbonized sand and vapors, rose up to the belly of his horse, which "stood motionless, struck with a panic of terror."

Daniel Drake in Cincinnati and Jared Brooks in Louisville kept careful records of the tremors as they occurred over a three-month period. The records show that the earthquakes that centered in what was then eastern New Madrid County in 1811–1812 were the biggest ones in recorded history to hit the North American continent. Only the quake that hit Anchorage, Alaska, in 1964 is believed to have been as strong or stronger. David Stewart believes that the five major quakes that occurred would have ranged between 8.3 and 8.5 on the Richter scale, while the Anchorage quake was registered as 8.8 or 8.9 on the scale. The New Madrid quakes, however, covered a larger area. Timothy Flint wrote that people living elsewhere in the country had little idea of the violence of the quakes because reports mainly described the buildings damaged or destroyed and the lives lost.

We pay more attention in the United States to the quakes in California because we hear more about the material destruction they cause and the number of people killed or injured by them. They also happen every few years in heavily populated areas and are strong enough to cause damage in such areas. The quake that hit San Francisco in 1906 is the one most Americans think of when they talk about early earthquakes. Many people were living close to the center of the quake in multistory buildings crowded into a relatively small area. As a result, many lives were lost and property damage was extensive. The quakes occurring in New Madrid County, however, affected more than one million square miles. California quakes usually affect no more than thirty thousand square miles.

Eliza Bryan wrote that the quake of January 23 was as fierce as those on December 16 and caused the same fear among the people and animals still in New Madrid. The smells, sounds, darkness, and movement of the first quakes were repeated. The tremors continued, with several shocks coming every day. On February 4, Bryan reported, the earth was in continual movement. The greatest quake of all occurred on February 7 at about

4 A.M. Bryan wrote that the river "seemed to recede from its banks, and its water gathered up like a mountain, leaving . . . boats . . . stranded on the sand." Some crew members escaped from their boats before the river came rushing back to overflow the land. Others drowned. The darkness, the noise, and the smells remembered were more horrifying than words can adequately describe.

Colonel John Shaw had been in the area when the first quakes struck. He was in New Madrid on the morning of February 7 and wrote that "people stopped only long enough to get their teams, and hurry in their families and some provisions. It was a matter of doubt among them, whether water or fire would . . . burst forth, and cover all the country." A camp was set up at Tywappety Hill about thirty miles north of New Madrid and seven miles west of the Mississippi River. Shaw heard that seventeen-year-old Betsey Masters was left behind by her parents and family when they fled. Her leg had been broken when one of the "weight-poles" of the roof of the cabin gave way. He went back and found "the poor girl upon a bed, as she had been left, with some water and corn bread within her reach." He cooked more food for her before he went back to the camp. "Miss Masters eventually recovered," he reported.

Local residents reported that fissures—long, deep cracks—appeared in the earth, one as long as five miles. Myron Fuller, a scientist who made a thorough investigation of the quake area in the early twentieth century, said that most of these fissures were from 600 to 700 feet long and wide enough to swallow a horse or cow. These fissures also sent sand, lukewarm water, and bad-smelling vapors into the air. The amount of water sent out of fissures at Little Prairie was enough to cover the ground for miles to a depth of from three to four feet.

The fissures all opened in the same direction, southwest to northeast. Each new break occurred in the same direction as the earlier ones. The deepest one measured twenty feet, and most were fairly narrow. Because they all opened in the same direction, the story arose that settlers cut down trees in advance so that they fell crosswise to the expected fissures. At the height of a quake, the story goes, frightened settlers would climb into the downed trees to keep from being swallowed by the earth. James Penick, writing about the quakes in 1976, argued that this story is probably not true: the idea of men felling trees during those first quakes and then getting the entire family to ride them through the next earthquake seems absurd. It seems absurd to me as well, but we have Ben Chartier's recollection telling almost the same story, and some scientists have accepted it. Myron Fuller, for example, believed the story.

Fuller said that the breaks in the earth nearest the riverbanks were the closest together, sometimes only a foot or so apart. The direction of the breaks is important because it suggests the direction of the earth waves. Fuller maintained that few of the breaks were more than twenty feet deep, and none were near the bottomless chasms feared by the settlers.

People who experienced the quakes firsthand said that during the three or four worst tremors they could not stand on their feet because of the rolling of the earth. Many people were dizzy and nauseated because of the constant motion. It may have been like being at sea during a severe storm. Others report that the air that had been clear became very dark in five minutes. Houses fifty feet away could not be seen. The quakes affected all of the senses: sight, sound, smell, taste, and touch. One settler reported that the cabin danced about as if it would fall on his family.

Reports from Survivors on the River

Falling riverbanks along the Mississippi River were common during and after the quakes. Timothy Flint reported that the graveyard at New Madrid fell into the river, and the river it-self flowed wildly in huge waves. According to author William Atkinson, the river changed from clear to a rusty brown color and became thick with mud and other bottom debris that came to the surface. Fissures opened under the river as they had on land so that the waters spouted and created whirlpools. The river rose from three to fifteen feet above its usual level. In some places it flowed at three times its normal speed, carrying trees, mud, and untended boats along with it. Navigation became very difficult. No one could count the deaths on the river, but people did tell of canoes empty of their occupants and boats of all kinds capsizing with no chance for the crews to be saved.

John Bradbury, the British botanist traveling the river on December 16, was south of New Madrid when he was awakened by a loud noise and violent movement of the boat. He could hear the crash of falling trees and the screams of wild birds. When the movement stopped, Bradbury said, "the perpendicular banks, both above and below us, began to fall into the river in such vast masses, as nearly to sink our boat."

Firmin La Roche, a boatman, was on the river north of New Madrid when the first quakes hit. "We believed we must surely die," he said. He described "a crash like thunder" and said "the boat turned upon its side." The air was thick with a smoke-like vapor, and there was a great deal of lightning. Father Joseph, a Catholic priest aboard with La Roche and his crew, gave last rites to the crew, who feared they would die. Father Joseph reported that as they neared New Madrid they saw houses burning, and "people were crowded out upon the hillside and were in great fear." The boat landed in New Madrid at about dawn. Father Joseph reported that a hickory tree fell upon the boat, killing one man and breaking La Roche's arm. Father Joseph went ashore and performed last rites for those settlers who requested them. He described the noise of the quake as muffled and groaning; sometimes, he said, it cracked and crashed like a great sheet of ice being broken.

William L. Pierce, another traveler on the river, was south of New Madrid at the time and said that sometimes air burst through to the river surface with a loud bang, and mud, sticks, and other debris were thrown above the surface. Trees that had been at the bottom of the river for ages were hurled into the air.

During the day, there were continued shocks and explosions like the rolling of thunder. The bed of the river was in constant turmoil; the noise of falling trees and the spouting river made it seem as if the world were coming to an end.

The *New Orleans*

The *New Orleans* was the first steamboat to travel the Mississippi River, and her first trip was in the fall of 1811. The *New*

The *New Orleans* was the first steamboat to travel the Mississippi. She reached the river during the earthquakes, at a time, James T. Lloyd wrote, when a steamboat "was to common observers, almost as great a wonder as a flying angel would be at present." Some people were frightened by the noise and smoke, but others hoped to be saved by the steamboat. It stopped at New Madrid and Little Prairie but could not take on passengers. (State Historical Society of Missouri, Columbia, from James T. Lloyd, *Lloyd's Steamboat Directory and Disasters on the Western Waters*)

Orleans was on the Ohio River headed toward New Madrid on the night of the first earthquake. The boat had been built by Nicholas Roosevelt with the help of Robert Fulton and Robert Livingston, steamboat pioneers. Nicholas Roosevelt would become the grand uncle of Theodore Roosevelt, who was born in 1858 and became president of the United States in 1901.

Nicholas Roosevelt had traveled the rivers with his wife, Lydia, on a flatboat for six months to learn the western rivers and their ways. The Mississippi River boatmen he talked with warned him that the Mississippi was not suitable for steamboats. He went ahead anyway, building the 116-foot, 410-ton *New Orleans* and traveling as captain from Pittsburgh with Lydia, then pregnant, and Rosetta, their two-year-old daughter. Lydia gave birth on October 30 to their second child, Henry Latrobe Roosevelt, while they were waiting at Louisville, Kentucky, for the Ohio River waters to rise.

The trip had been uneventful until they were near Louisville, where they were held up for three weeks because of low waters. When water levels made it possible to navigate again, they took on the waterfall west of Louisville with no problems. They were near Henderson, Kentucky, when the first quake occurred. The crew expected the boat to sink because of the turmoil of the waters. They could hear mud banks crashing into the river. By dawn they could see trees three feet in diameter being thrown into the water, but they continued on their way.

Roosevelt and his crew reached New Madrid on December 19 and went ashore briefly. They noted that most of the chimneys were down. The noise of their boat and its billowing smoke added to the distress and confusion of the people on shore. Some residents tried to get passage aboard the boat to escape from the quakes; others were more frightened of the steamboat than of the quakes. The boat left without taking on passengers.

The *New Orleans* continued south, and members of the crew had to go ashore almost every night to cut firewood needed for fuel for the next day. Whether on land or on the river, they were nervous, afraid that they would perish. The land shook regularly, and on the river they saw broken boats and debris along the entire trip. They continued south to Natchez, Mississippi, even though the river had changed so much that it was almost impossible to navigate. Eventually they made their way to New Orleans.

Matthis Speed

Matthis Speed was part of a boat crew on the Mississippi River on February 6; his crew tied their boat with another one to a willow bar east of New Madrid that night. They were awakened at about 3 A.M. by an earthquake. Speed said that it was louder and scarier than they could describe. The closest he could come to describing the noises was to compare them to the constant shooting of heavy cannon. The crew saw that the bar they had tied to was sinking. They cut the two boats loose and moved them closer to the middle of the river to protect themselves and the boats from the trees and riverbanks that were falling into the water.

The river was in such a frenzy that it seemed at any minute their boat would be overthrown. At dawn, Speed said, the river appeared to be almost black with something like the dust of coal. He admitted that at this point he was in such a state of alarm that he was not certain about the length and height of new falls that appeared in the Mississippi River, but he and others reported that falls appeared between islands 9 and 10 on the river, very close to New Madrid. (The islands are numbered in order beginning at Cairo, Illinois, where the Ohio River enters the Mississippi, and going south. Island 9 is almost due east of New Madrid; island 10 is about six river miles south of island 9.)

Speed's boat crew landed at New Madrid near breakfast time, and what they saw there did not comfort them. Speed reported that the banks of the river had dropped about twelve feet. Few houses remained untouched: some had lost their roofs and chimneys, and others were destroyed entirely. The people of

New Madrid had left their homes and were camping in shelters made of light boards because they were afraid of being under a roof or anything heavy that could injure them if it fell. They had canoes near their camps so they could be ready to leave if the river rose again.

Speed and the boat crew stayed in New Madrid until February 12; shocks continued, accompanied by rumbling sounds that to him sounded like far-off thunder. Most of the surface of the land had dropped about twelve feet and was even with the tops of the boats in the river. Before the quakes, New Madrid overlooked the Mississippi from bluffs. The six days that Speed was in New Madrid about twenty boats landed. The boat crews he talked to recalled the fury of the river and the falls much as he did.

Members of one of the boat crews coming downriver the morning that Speed landed in New Madrid were so afraid of the falls that they took a canoe from their boat and tried to land on the island. Two men got onto the island; the other two men made for the western bank in the canoe. As they neared the bank, they saw that the island was shaking violently. One of the men they had left on the island threw himself into the river and swam for the canoe. They turned the canoe and picked up the man; these three made their way to New Madrid by land.

The fourth man, stranded on the island, was picked up three days later by a crew in another canoe and brought to New Madrid. There he told a riveting story of his survival. The island was shaken regularly and often, he said; sand, coal, and luke-warm water were thrown up from the earth. He reported that frequent lights appeared (when an earthquake is large enough to squeeze quartz crystals, which are present in most soils, the resulting voltage emits visible light). At one point he held onto a tree to keep from being thrown to the ground. He and the tree fell into a fissure that opened up under them. He was injured in the fall, and the break was too deep and its sides too steep for him to get out. He had to walk along the bottom of the fissure to a place where the sloping side allowed him to crawl to dry ground.

The River

The river sometimes receded from its banks, leaving small boats on the bare sand. It would then rise fifteen or twenty feet straight up, flowing over its banks; sometimes it flowed backward. Because of this violent movement of the water, the boats that had been stranded would be torn away and sometimes sent up small creeks. When the river receded, it was with such force that it took away stands of trees that had been on its banks. Fish were thrown up on the ground, and there were many boat wrecks. Eliza Bryan reported that one wrecked boat had held a woman and six children; all of them were lost to the river.

The quake of February 7, the largest of all, is now estimated at perhaps 8.5 or more on the Richter scale. It caused the Mississippi River to run backward for a few hours between islands 8 and 10. This quake created the two waterfalls, one less than a mile upstream from New Madrid. Settlers watched with horror what was happening there. The waterfalls remained only two or three days, but they allowed the river to drop about six feet into a mile of shallow rapids. Within that time, settlers saw thirty boats come over the falls. Of those, twenty-eight were overcome by the waters and capsized. There were few survivors. People on shore could hear the victims scream for help and could do nothing. There were nineteen boats tied up at New Madrid on February 7. They were all torn away from their docks and swept southward, never to be seen again.

The worst of the quakes caused the river to boil and heave, with large waves hitting one bank and then the other. Some people said the river opened up and the water disappeared into great holes. Others said that spouts of water shot up from the river. The river was covered with the wreckage of boats.

Animals

Eliza Bryan mentioned in her letter the cries of the animals, both tame and wild, following the quake. Their noises added to the confusion of sounds, smells, and movement. There was apparently a large migration of squirrels at the Ohio River prior to the quakes. James Penick tells of how the wild animals moved together during the quakes in great migrations. Bears, wolves, deer, and other animals that were usually enemies showed no sign of enmity.

William Atkinson reports in *The Next New Madrid Earthquake* that animal behavior prior to earthquakes can be bizarre. For example, in 373 B.C. rats, snakes, and weasels left Helice, Greece, in droves. Five days later, Helice was destroyed by an earthquake. Dogs barked and howled all night before the San Francisco earthquake of 1906; the next day, horses tore loose from their stables, and cows ran in panic. The Chinese, according to Atkinson, have been studying animal behavior for 3,000 years. Because they see odd behavior of animals as predictions of earthquakes, they have responded by clearing crowded cities before quakes. They believe that over the years this response to animal behavior may have saved a million lives.

Animals may indicate in a number of ways that an earthquake is on its way. Animals that burrow are more sensitive than those that live aboveground, and small animals seem to be more sensitive than large ones. Ducks will not go into the water, fish jump above the water's surface, and pigeons will not nest. Larger animals also show strange behavior, and that may be the reason Ben Chartier's father turned the hogs out at the first quake in Little Prairie.

Following the disaster of the New Madrid earthquakes, settlers, hunters and trappers, Indians, and even wild animals left the area. It was a long time before the people and the land in southeastern Missouri healed.

CHAPTER 3

The Earthquake's Reach

"Chimneys fell in Cincinnati. Sidewalks buckled in Baltimore. Church bells rang in Boston."

— David Stewart and Ray Knox,
The Earthquake that Never Went Away

The New Madrid earthquakes affected an area of about one million square miles. Some places were affected more severely than others. Tremors could be felt in two-thirds of what was then the United States and its territories, from the Atlantic on the east to the Rocky Mountains on the west. The quakes were also felt north to Upper Canada and south to Mexico and Cuba. They were felt strongly at Charleston, South Carolina, and Savannah, Georgia, on the Atlantic coast, a distance of some 600 miles. The Otoe Indians on the Nebraska-Kansas border felt the shocks; they were also about 600 miles from the earthquake site, but in the opposite direction.

Mississippi Valley

St. Louis, about 200 miles north of the first epicenter, felt the first tremors at about 2:15 A.M. on December 16. People were awakened by the rattling of windows and doors. They reported a rumbling sound, as if several carriages were passing over the

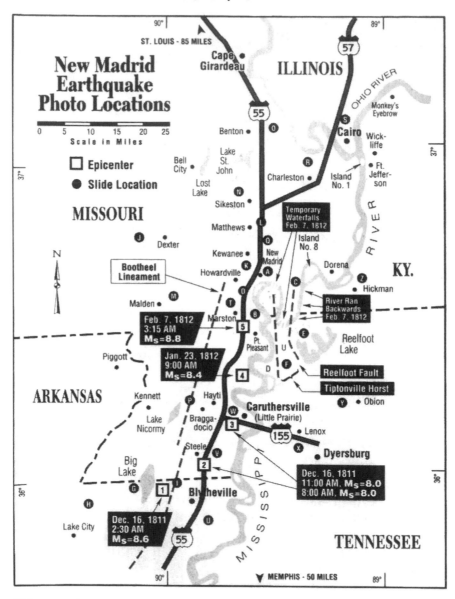

This map shows the epicenters and times of the New Madrid earthquakes. (courtesy David Stewart and Ray Knox from *The Earthquake that Never Went Away*, 1993)

pavement. They also felt the later shocks of that morning, each of which lasted from several seconds to two minutes. Some chimneys were destroyed and some stone houses split. Caged birds fell from their perches, and many people vacated their homes. William Atkinson reports that a thick, hazy fog hung over the city. It is important to note that the location of St. Louis puts it outside the direct reach of the fault line; the line moves in a southwest to northeast direction from current Blytheville, Arkansas, to Cairo, Illinois. St. Louis is slightly west of that line and north of Cairo, the northernmost edge of the fault line.

Atkinson reports that about fifty miles north of New Madrid at Jackson, Missouri, the tremors destroyed large trees, fences, and brick buildings. Haze and dark clouds blurred the sun for three days. In Kaskaskia, Illinois, closer to the fault line, he says that "the earth rolled and waved violently. The church steeple bent, and the bell clanged loudly." Cattle ran through the streets in fear.

As far south as what is now Vicksburg, Mississippi, the river claimed its banks, and islands had deep fissures and large sinkholes. Sinkholes, also called sand blows, were formed during the quakes when sand, coal, quartz, and other materials were forced out of the earth. What remains are circular depressions that are filled with sand or quicksand and ringed with carbonized wood and sand. Twenty acres of land next to the Mississippi River near Piney River, Tennessee, sank, so that the tops of trees there were level with the land next to the sunken area. In other parts of Tennessee, people reported that shocks came daily for the rest of the year. In Columbia, Tennessee (170 miles to the east), residents claimed that the shocks lasted from ten to fifteen minutes. In Christian County, Kentucky (120 miles to the east of New Madrid), a clear spring became muddy and stayed muddy for hours. Roads from New Madrid to settlements in Arkansas 200 miles away became impassable with the first quake. The distance was lengthened to 300 miles for those who needed to make the trip.

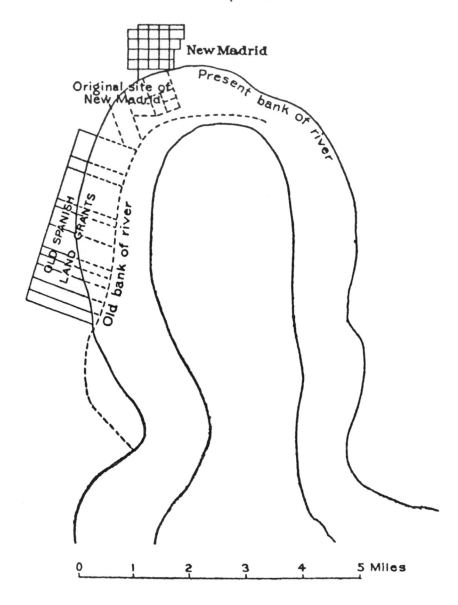

The curve of the Mississippi River where New Madrid is located is called the New Madrid Bend (also called Kentucky Bend), Mississippi River. New Madrid is now located almost due north of its location before the earthquake. This drawing shows the channel of the Mississippi River in about 1912 and the river's course before 1811.

Timothy Dudley of Jacksonville, Illinois, recounts a story told to him by James Ritchie fifty years after the earthquake. A family named Curran, he says, was moving from New Madrid to Arkansas and lost some cattle on the way. LeRoy, the Currans' teenage son, asked to take a pony back to look for the animals. Neither LeRoy Curran nor the cattle were ever seen again. Dudley adds that at the time of the quakes, Ritchie said the air was so smoky that the Kentucky shore, one mile away from New Madrid, could not be seen.

In 1912 Myron Fuller made a detailed study of the earthquakes and the effects they had outside the New Madrid area. His record of the quakes, published in a bulletin by the United States Geological Survey, is a valuable document for those studying the New Madrid fault line and the quakes that happened in 1811–1812. The direction of movement recorded during the quakes seems to have varied somewhat depending on the location. Fuller points out that seismic measuring devices, which are used to gauge the intensity of earthquakes, were in a very primitive state in 1811. Instruments were often handmade, pendulums and the like. Fuller also notes that there is general agreement in the written records about the direction the quakes moved following the most severe tremors.

Fuller found that the first quake was felt at New Orleans, 500 miles south of the center, but the shock was not severe. Natchez, Mississippi, 300 miles south of the center, felt four shocks the morning of December 16. Some plastered walls cracked, items fell from shelves, and some clocks stopped. Some of the riverbanks at Natchez fell, and the river was stirred up. Treetops waved from side to side, but no one reported noise caused by the quakes. The lack of noise is unusual; in most places, people reported loud and frightening noises.

The Midwest

At Jefferson, Indiana, temperatures warmed for several days after the earthquakes, and the air was smoky. Fuller found that at Vincennes, Indiana, about 200 miles from the quakes' center, the first shock was so severe that people were afraid that their homes would come down. This same fear was recorded at Lebanon, Ohio, northeast of Cincinnati and more than 400 miles from the fault line. At Lebanon, movement was horizontal and of such strength that people ran from their homes.

According to Fuller, Daniel Drake, a physician, left the only scientific report of the quakes as they occurred in Cincinnati. Drake noted that at 2:24 A.M. on December 16 the first quake hit Cincinnati with a quick, rocking motion and lasted some six or seven minutes. Its violence moved furniture, opened doors that were not latched, and tore down some chimneys. The shock of January 23 hit at about 9 A.M., causing repeated waving of the earth, in a movement going from south-southwest to north-northeast. Some people became dizzy from the movement.

The quake on February 7, Drake reported, hit in Cincinnati at 3:45 A.M. and was the most damaging of all. More chimneys were shaken down, breaks appeared in brick walls, and people suffered more dizziness and nausea than ever. On February 8 at 10:40 A.M., there was another shock, but this one was different: The earlier ones had moved horizontally. This one made more of a vertical motion. Drake said that some people heard a noise before the earlier shocks hit, and some did not. With the last shock, Drake heard a strange, dull, rushing sound from the southwest about five seconds before the shaking of the earth began. Drake also recorded the many lighter shocks in Cincinnati.

Louisville, Kentucky

Cincinnati, Ohio, and Louisville, Kentucky, were the largest settlements west of the Allegheny Mountains and the largest cities near the earthquake center. At Louisville, according to Fuller, Jared Brooks had built pendulums in different lengths to detect horizontal movements of the earth. He also built a number of springs to record the vertical movements. His instruments measured 1,874 quakes and aftershocks from December

16, 1811, to March 15, 1812. Louisville is about 250 miles from the earthquake's center. Brooks noted in his charts the date, time of day, weather conditions, and intensity of each shock.

Brooks ranked the quakes at Louisville into six categories. Of the 1,874 shocks reported, 8 were violent, 10 were severe, and 35 were moderate. The others he classified as either those that people were generally aware of or those felt only by sensitive people who were not in motion at the time. These last also caused movement of some objects that would move in a brisk wind.

Brooks was an engineer and a surveyor; his records are thorough, precise, and believed to be accurate. He reports that when the first quake hit Louisville at 2:15 A.M. on December 16 it lasted 3½ to 4 minutes, increasing in strength at first and then subsiding. The second one, just after 7 A.M., moved the earth for about 10 minutes. The damage was extensive; chimneys, gable ends, and parapets were thrown down from buildings. Houses and other large objects moved violently and in different directions. "It seemed as if the surface of the earth was afloat and set in motion by a slight application of immense power, but . . . broken by a sudden cross shove [with] all order destroyed," Brooks wrote.

John James Audubon, famed painter and naturalist, recorded a dramatic story of his experience with the quakes. He claimed that they occurred in November in mid-afternoon, but the November date could easily have been a mistake in his journal dating. We are not certain how much time passed between the time of the incident and the time he recorded his experience. Author David Logsdon believes that the quake Audubon experienced was actually the one on January 23. In January, Audubon and Vincent Nolte, a merchant, had traveled together down the Ohio River to Kentucky, where they separated, each going his own way. They report similar experiences.

The fact that none of the bigger quakes occurred in the afternoon has bothered some people about Audubon's report of the quake he felt. However, he may have been close enough to the fault line to have felt one of the smaller quakes. Jared Brooks's

John James Audubon, noted American naturalist, recorded his experience during the January 23 earthquake in Kentucky. This bronze memorial, on the site in Henderson where Audubon had a store, was dedicated in 1925. (Henderson County Genealogical and Historical Society, Henderson, Kentucky)

charts of the quakes in Louisville note several afternoon quakes that ranged in strength from moderate to violent.

Audubon wrote that he was riding his horse through the Barrens of Kentucky when he heard a noise that made him suspect a tornado was nearing. He wanted to get to shelter and spurred his horse to move faster, but the horse groaned, hung his head, and stood stock-still, legs splayed under him. The horse continued to groan. At that moment, the ground began to rise and fall like the ruffled waters of a lake. Audubon found himself rocking "to and fro like a child in a cradle" as both horse and rider felt the earthquake. The noise Audubon mentions is similar to that recorded by Drake in Cincinnati.

Vincent Nolte reported a similar experience. He was riding through a forest between Frankfort and Louisville, Kentucky. The trees had been heaving and waving in a strange pattern, and his horse suddenly stood stock-still. When Nolte tried to make him move, the horse seemed seized with terror, and it "was some time before he fell into his usual pace."

The Great Lakes Region

Fuller found several accounts of shocks in the Great Lakes area. James Witherall, a Detroit judge, reported that prior to a tremor on February 3, the temperature had risen for several hours. He reported shocks through February 8, with the last one moving the earth vertically. Earlier shocks had been horizontal. Another judge in the Michigan Territory reported that there had been nine tremors from the earthquake, four of which he felt. Later, following a trip to upper Canada, he noted that people there had also reported nine shocks.

Reports from the East

In Washington, D.C., almost 800 miles from the earthquake's center, people were awakened near 3 A.M. on December 16 to the noise of their doors slamming and windows moving. More tremors followed, moving tassels of curtains and the crystal pendants of light fixtures. Water pitchers, set out on washstands for early morning washups, rattled in their basins. There was such noise with the movement that some people thought robbers had entered their homes. Later in the day, a man was standing and writing at his desk in the third story of a brick building near Capitol Hill. He felt his body moving and became ill from the motion. When he looked at the walls, he saw that a mirror was in motion. Other Washington residents reported similar happenings.

South of Washington, D.C., in Richmond, Virginia, residents reported the same kind of movement and noise. They, like the people of Washington, feared that robbers were in their homes. In one large home, bells were set ringing on upper and lower floors. East of Richmond, in Norfolk, people reported that clocks stopped, doors rattled, and anything hanging from the ceiling moved to and fro.

Lawmakers in session at the statehouse in Raleigh, North Carolina, became so alarmed when the building shook that they adjourned. They thought that the quake had occurred in their state; it was actually almost 700 miles away.

In Columbia, South Carolina, the air was filled with vapors that lasted for some time. These vapors were apparently not so offensive as those closer to the centers of the quakes, where people reported very bad smells.

Light flashes similar to those seen near New Madrid were reported at Savannah, Georgia, where a flash preceded the first quake. In North Carolina, in Knoxville, Tennessee, and in St. Louis there were several light flashes reported.

Land and River Changes

Reelfoot Lake

One of the lasting effects of the quake occurred across the river from Missouri, in Tennessee. Reelfoot Lake, in western Tennessee in the eastern part of the quake area, was created by the quakes. Fuller reports that the region was low and wet before the earthquakes, but it became much deeper following them. Before the quakes, Reelfoot Creek flowed through the area and into the Obion River. Afterward, there was a lake 18 miles long, as wide as 5 miles in some places, and from 5 to 20 feet deep. Located about 5 miles west of Tiptonville, Tennessee, it covers 13,000 acres. Now Running Reelfoot Bayou flows from the south end of Reelfoot Lake to the Obion.

The lake remained almost unused for 50 or more years after the quakes and became a fertile breeding ground for bass, crappie, catfish, and other freshwater fish. It is now a popular fishing

This photograph shows Reelfoot Lake, Tennessee, in about 1912. The cypress trees shown in the photograph were covered with water during the New Madrid earthquake. Some are still alive today and up to 300 years old. (*U.S. Geological Survey, Bulletin 494*, plate 7, courtesy State Historical Society of Missouri, Columbia)

and camping area. It is also home to two National Wildlife Refuges totalling more than 10,000 acres and attracts some 220 bird species, including many waterfowl and the bald eagle.

Before the quakes created Reelfoot Lake, according to Myron Fuller, the area had been heavily wooded. The trees remained upright for the most part for many years, but most were eventually killed by the rising waters. Stewart and Knox believe that Reelfoot Lake began forming with the January 23 quake, when huge sand boils constricted Reelfoot Creek. The quake of February 7 brought on the final stages of the lake's formation. Cypress trees that were partly submerged by the quakes can still be seen.

Other Changes

Stewart and Knox report that the December 16 quakes also formed Big Lake on the border between Missouri and Arkansas, very near the epicenter of the first quake. Like Reelfoot, Big Lake is very popular as a fishing and camping area today. Many other lakes were created as well. Even though most of them were shallow, they lasted more than 100 years following the quakes. In the western part of the affected area, the bed of the St. Francis River in Missouri was lowered.

During the January 23 quake, trees, riverbanks, and other debris falling into the river caused such enormous swells that rumors still persist that the Mississippi and the Ohio rivers ran backward for several days. Stewart and Knox maintain that the Mississippi River did run backward, but only one section did so, and it was only for a period of a few hours.

Great waves occurred in the Mississippi River from slides of mud along the bluffs. Islands and shoals disappeared, and others formed at new places. One of the islands to disappear on December 16 was island 94, upstream from what would become Vicksburg, Mississippi. A boat crew led by Captain Paul Sarpy of St. Louis was on its way to New Orleans on December 15. They had intended to stop at island 94 but discovered that river pirates were living on the island. Changing channels, falling riverbanks, and underwater trees and debris were natural hazards to river traffic. River pirates also were a serious threat to Mississippi River boat crews. Pirates had been harassing crews and robbing riverboats for as long as the river had been used for trade. The pirates were not aware of Captain Sarpy's boat, which the crew decided to tie up for a few hours.

That night, Captain Sarpy and his crew quietly untied their boat and drifted farther down the river to another island, where they could tie up, keep watch on island 94, and be prepared if the pirates tried to attack. The earthquake in the early morning changed everything. When the fog and vapors cleared somewhat the next day, the men saw that island 94 was gone, along with the pirates. Both island and pirates were victims of the quake.

Over an area of 30,000 square miles the land surface was lowered from six to fifteen feet; over a much smaller area the land was raised by similar amounts.

Five towns in three states disappeared as well. Missouri's Little Prairie was flooded out in the first quakes; the residents left and did not return. Only the Walker and Covington families remained, and for forty-five years the town was known as "Lost Village." In 1857 a new town in that location was laid out and named Caruthersville for Representative James Caruthers of Madison County. Big Prairie, Arkansas, was flooded out at the same time, and its settlers left. Helena, Arkansas, was later located near the site of Big Prairie. An Indian village about eight miles south of New Madrid was destroyed by the river; Point Pleasant now stands at that location. Fort Jefferson, Kentucky, had been founded in 1789 to protect settlers from Indian uprisings but was largely uninhabited in 1811. The quakes proved it to be a place of unstable soils and landslides, so it was not rebuilt. New Madrid, too, disappeared into the river following the quakes of February 7.

Reports show that the quakes were felt in twenty-eight states and the District of Columbia. Eyewitness accounts, though some may be faulty, are too numerous and consistent not to be believed. In addition, geological evidence suggests that the New Madrid earthquake was "The Big One."

CHAPTER 4

After the Disaster

"This district, formerly so level, rich, and beautiful,

had the most melancholy of all aspects of decay."

— Timothy Flint, in *"I Was There!" In the New Madrid Earthquakes of 1811–12*

Scientists believe that the epicenter of the first quake in December 1811 was about sixty miles south of New Madrid, close to what is now Blytheville, Arkansas. New Madrid was the most populated town in the area, a thriving market town, with stores, trading posts, and active river traffic and commerce. The town's dominance in the area, combined with the fact that the quakes originated in New Madrid County, account for the quakes' being called the "New Madrid earthquake." The underlying fault line is still called the "New Madrid Seismic Zone."

In 1812 the Territory of New Orleans became the state of Louisiana, and Congress changed the name of the Upper Louisiana Territory to the Territory of Missouri. The five Missouri counties, named for the major Spanish and French towns on the eastern side of the territory, had a total population of less than 10,000 in 1812. St. Louis had the largest number of residents:

St. Louis	3,149
Cape Girardeau	2,026
Ste. Genevieve	1,701
New Madrid	1,548
St. Charles	1,096

Ten years later, in 1822, 70,647 people lived within the newly formed state of Missouri, but the population of New Madrid County had been reduced by almost one-third, from 1,548 in 1812 to 1,155. *Goodspeed's History of Southeast Missouri* reports that following the quakes only two families remained in the town of New Madrid. The others left behind their cattle and most of their household goods in their hurry to leave the area. The Delaware Indians left the New Madrid area in 1812 and settled in northwest Missouri at Chillicothe, a Shawnee word meaning "large town where we live." A Shawnee village in Ohio had the same name. Stewart and Knox report that at the time of the first quakes, one Shawnee tribe lived in a village named Chillicothe north of Cape Girardeau. The Shawnee village was more than twice the size of Cape Girardeau in 1811.

The only place where growth was reported in the area most affected by the earthquake was in the membership of the Methodist church. The Methodists had established a church in New Madrid in 1810. During 1812, church membership grew by more than 50 percent in the nine-state area where the quakes had been felt. Methodist membership within the earthquake area in 1811 was 30,741; in 1812, membership had grown to 45,983 in the same area. This happened at a time when Methodist membership in the rest of the United States grew by less than 1 percent.

Ministers were glad to see the increase in church membership; some saw an advantage in the fear that sinners suffered during the quakes. Historian Walter Brownlow Posey wrote about the changing approaches to evangelism following the earthquakes. He suggested that it was not surprising that people saw the wrath

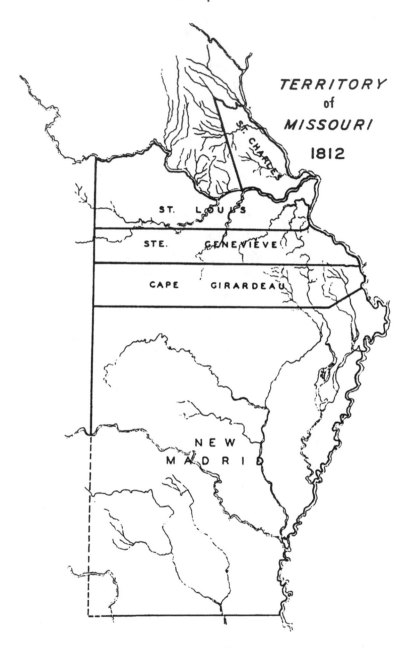

Map of the Territory of Missouri, 1812. The Louisiana Territory became the Territory of Missouri in 1812. (from the *Official Manual* for 1945–1946; original map from the State Historical Society of Missouri, Columbia)

of God in the quakes that shook the earth for three months. He told the story of one minister, James B. Finley, who said that landslidings were a reminder of backslidings. On one occasion during a quake, Finley jumped on a table and cried, "For the Great day of His wrath is come, and who shall be able to stand?"

Some ministers called these new converts "earthquake Christians" and questioned their sincerity. But evidence shows that several ministers openly rejoiced at the fear and trembling of "sinners" who feared facing their Maker. "It was a time of great terror for sinners," wrote Finley.

The New Madrid Claims

The destruction of such a large area in and around New Madrid left many people without homes or usable land. After the quakes, most of the land was under water or damaged by sand boils and was therefore unsuitable for farming. The natural disaster affected hundreds of families, leaving them without homes or a way to make a living.

An earthquake in Venezuela in March of 1812 damaged the cities of Caracas and La Guaira and killed 20,000 people. The United States government set aside $50,000 for the aid of the survivors. At that time, no government aid had been extended to victims of the New Madrid earthquake. In January of 1814 representatives of the Missouri Territory asked the federal government to show the same concern for its own citizens that it had shown to victims in Venezuela.

Finally, in 1815, Congress came to the relief of those whose homes and lands had been lost in the earthquakes through a law that became known as the "New Madrid claims." Settlers in the earthquake area of the Missouri Territory who had lost their homes and acreages were offered the chance to settle on any other land in Missouri that was still open to settlement. No claims were to exceed 640 acres, but landowners could claim an amount equal to what they had lost in southeast Missouri.

Submerged trees in the Mississippi seen from the levee at New Madrid.
Across the river is Kentucky. (photo by the author)

Unfortunately, most of the original settlers had already left
the area. Communication between the country's capital and the
western lands often took many weeks, so many quake victims
did not learn about the government program until much later.
Thus, the people the law was intended to help often did not
know anything about it until after they had sold or traded their
claims at pitifully low prices. Land sharks came into the area
as soon as they learned about the government program. They
bought up as many claims as they could so that they could
claim other lands within the state. Evidence also shows that
some of the original settlers sold their land more than once
when they learned about the claims. According to Myron Fuller,
516 claim certificates were issued, but only 20 were used by
original landowners. The rest were taken by persons who saw an
opportunity to gain a financial advantage. Historian Lucien Carr

wrote, "Three hundred and eighty-four [claims] were held by persons who resided in St. Louis." Some St. Louisans possessed more than 20 claims each. They paid $40 to $60 per claim. Some claims were as large as 640 acres.

Governor William Clark, who had gained fame as part of the Lewis and Clark expedition, made money on the government decision to allow quake victims to exchange damaged land for the same amount of land elsewhere in the public domain. Shortly after passage of the act, Clark authorized his deputies to purchase land titles. The amount of cheating and thievery was so widespread that the term *New Madrid claim* came to mean fraud and theft.

The New Madrid that George Morgan had named for the capital of Spain was taken over by the river. The busy market town Morgan planned lasted less than twenty-five years before it fell victim to the fault far beneath its surface.

In 1811, New Madrid County stretched almost across the Missouri Territory to within thirty miles of the state's current western border. It reached about sixty miles south in an almost straight line into what is now Arkansas. This area now contains twenty counties in Missouri alone.

When Missouri became a state in 1821, there was a move to draw the southern border straight across and parallel to the state's northern border on the same latitude as the Kentucky-Tennessee boundary east of the Mississippi River. It made a certain amount of sense and would have been in keeping with the borders of many later western states that were not determined by rivers and ocean rims. However, John Hardeman Walker owned the land south of the proposed border in southeastern New Madrid County, land between the Mississippi and St. Francis rivers. He had settled in the Missouri Territory in 1810, had developed strong ties to his Missouri neighbors to the north, and did not want to live in Arkansas. Walker objected strongly to the placement of his property in the territory to

Map of Missouri, 1821. Missouri became the twenty-fourth state in the
Union in August 1821. (from the *Official Manual* for 1945–1946, courtesy
State Historical Society of Missouri, Columbia)

the south, and he was powerful enough to persuade legislators
making border decisions to include his land in Missouri. It is
because of John Hardeman Walker that we have the jagged border in our state's southeastern corner that forms the "Missouri
Bootheel."

CHAPTER 5

Earthquake Predictions

"Will the earthquakes come again? Yes. This is an active seismic zone."

— Carolyn V. Platt, "Nightmare on the Mississippi," in *Timeline*

The New Madrid Seismic Zone is about 150 miles long, reaching from near Marked Tree, Arkansas, on the south through southeastern Missouri to near Metropolis, Illinois, on the north. The zone is believed to be about 50 miles wide.

A geologic fault is a break in a rock formation caused by a shifting of the earth's crust. Primary faults, which lie far beneath the earth's surface, cannot be seen. They cause earthquakes by a sudden shift. Secondary, or surface, faults are caused by earthquakes and are often visible.

Today the intensity of earthquakes is generally measured according to the Richter scale, which records the magnitude of a quake as it occurs (see Appendix 2 for information on the Richter scale). Each 0.2-unit increase in the scale indicates twice the power of the mark before it. Thus, an earthquake measuring 8.4 on the Richter scale would be two times stronger than one measuring 8.2. An earthquake measuring 8.0 on the Richter scale would be 32 times stronger than one measuring 7.0. David Stewart points out that earthquakes cannot be measured with total accuracy. The measurement can be off by as much as 0.2

The New Madrid Fault System "extends southward from the area of
Charleston, Missouri, and Cairo, Illinois, through New Madrid and
Caruthersville, following Interstate 55 to Blytheville and on down to
Marked Tree, Arkansas," according to the Center for Earthquake Studies in
Cape Girardeau. It lies in five states and crosses the Mississippi River in three
places. (map courtesy *Geotimes,* American Geological Institute, Alexandria,
Virginia)

or 0.3 units. This discrepancy takes on greater significance when
we know a 0.2-unit variation is not a small difference. Stewart
also notes that the Richter scale and our use of it are continually
developing.

Earthquakes of moderate size can cause great injury and damage if they occur in an area with a large population and where
buildings are close together, as they often are in cities. In El
Salvador, for example, in October 1986, an earthquake occurred
that measured only 5.4 on the Richter scale; yet the effects of
it killed 1,000 people in the city of San Salvador and caused
extensive property damage. In September 1985, an earthquake

in Mexico measuring 8.1 on the Richter scale had its epicenter 250 miles away from Mexico City, but the effects of it killed 10,000 people in that city.

Otto Nuttli, a professor of geophysics at St. Louis University, has given considerable thought to the New Madrid fault line and the effect an earthquake as powerful as the ones of 1811–1812 could have on the area now. Scientists believe that the five major earthquakes that occurred in 1811–1812 would have surpassed 8.0 on the Richter scale if the device had been available at the time. Such quakes today resulting from the New Madrid fault could cause major damage in Missouri, Illinois, Indiana, Ohio, Arkansas, Tennessee, and Kentucky. Memphis, for example, is only twenty-five miles from the fault line and has a population of over half a million people. Memphis would be especially vulnerable because it is built on semi-consolidated rock that is covered with soft and crumbly soil and floodplain deposits. Such soil can turn to liquid in an earthquake, as it did in New Madrid and Little Prairie. Concrete highways would buckle, and bridges and brick buildings would collapse. Property damage in Memphis, if such a quake occurred, could be in the billions of dollars. Many of the city's residents could lose their lives.

Small earthquakes, those with magnitudes of less than 3.0 on the Richter scale, occur about 200 times a year in the central United States. They usually go unnoticed, detected only by very sensitive instruments. Earthquakes of 3.0–5.0 magnitude occur about six times a year in the same area. Sometimes during one of these quakes, things will slide from a table or shelf. People can feel the movement, but no serious damage occurs.

Nuttli discounts the folklore that small earthquakes relieve pressure on the earth and therefore prevent larger ones. He compares this theory to believing that minor chest pains can deter a massive heart attack. Both small earthquakes and minor chest pains are symptoms of something wrong; in one case it is with the earth, in the other with the body.

Earthquakes measuring 5.0 or more on the Richter scale are possible anywhere in the Midwest. Four have occurred since the late 1960s. Quakes measuring just under 6.0 on the Richter scale occur 3 or 4 times every century in the Midwest. They can cause moderate damage at the epicenter of the quake and mild damage as far as 20 to 30 miles away.

Quakes measuring from above 6.0 to a bit over 7.0 on the Richter scale occur in the Midwest only about once every 80 years; the last one was in 1895. There is a 50 percent chance that a quake of this magnitude will occur by the year 2000 and a 90 percent chance that one will take place by the year 2040. Quakes measuring 7.5 to about 8.0 happen perhaps every 200 to 300 years. A brochure published by the Center for Earthquake Studies at Cape Girardeau predicts that there is a 25 percent chance of a quake this strong by the year 2040. It is important to remember the rule about 0.2 units here; with each 0.2-unit gain on the Richter scale, the magnitude is doubled.

No quakes over 7.0 have been recorded in the central United States since equipment to measure earthquakes in this way was created; the aftershocks of the 1811–1812 quakes are believed to be the only ones to exceed this level of magnitude since Europeans settled in the Midwest. Nuttli believes that earthquakes of such magnitude might do structural damage over a large area and minor damage several hundred miles from the epicenter.

The most powerful earthquake in the central United States in this century occurred in 1968 near Eldorado, in southeastern Illinois. Eldorado is on the Wabash Valley fault, and the quake had a reading of 5.3 or 5.4 on the Richter scale and a Mercalli intensity rating of VII (see Appendix 1 for information on the Mercalli scale). It was felt in twenty-four states, covering an area of more than half a million square miles. Plaster cracked, windows broke, and heavy objects within buildings moved. Buildings swayed in Omaha, Chicago, and Memphis. People in high-rise buildings as far away as Boston reported feeling the movement.

Of the suspected seismic zones in the Midwest, the New Madrid Seismic Zone has been the strongest to date and seems to pose the greatest threat of powerful quakes in the future. The

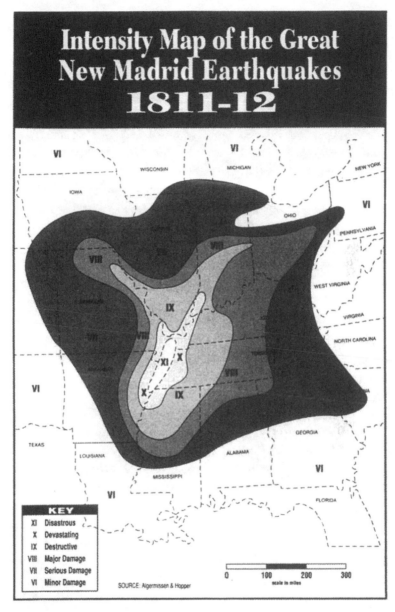

Mercalli scale intensity map of the New Madrid earthquake. The "earthquake" was a series of over 2,000 shocks in a five-month period; five shocks were 8.0 or more in magnitude based on the Richter scale. (courtesy David Stewart and Ray Knox from *The Earthquake that Never Went Away*, 1993)

number of tremors occurring in 1811–1812 in a three-month period is equal to the number that occurred in southern California in the forty-year period from 1932 to 1972. Earthquake potential in the central United States is easily equal to that of California. California has more quakes, but those in the Midwest cause damage to larger areas.

Midwestern earthquakes pose greater danger to a larger area than earthquakes west of the Rocky Mountains because the soil and rock structures in the two areas are substantially different. The bedrock of the West does not transmit seismic energy efficiently because the rocks are hot, or at least warm, and young. East of the Rockies, the bedrock is older and transmits seismic energy very efficiently. Thus, the damage caused by the energy of an earthquake in older bedrock is transmitted over greater distances. The earthquake in San Francisco in 1906, for example, caused severe damage within the city, but it only moderately affected an area of about 60,000 square miles. The New Madrid quakes, by contrast, *strongly* affected an area of 50,000 square miles, *moderately* affected an area of one million square miles, and *to a lesser extent* affected an area of two million square miles.

Faults in the rocks of the Midwest show that earthquakes of large magnitude have occurred for several thousand years. One problem in predicting future earthquake activity is that we have limited knowledge. We have accurate records only of the tremors that have occurred since the first European explorers came to the area, about 300 years ago. That is not long enough to enable scientists to predict earthquakes with any certainty. The earliest written report cites an earthquake near Memphis in 1699. A later quake was reported by a Moravian missionary in 1776. Still others were reported in 1779 and 1792 in Kentucky, and quakes near Kaskaskia in southwest Illinois were recorded in 1795 and 1804.

Sir Charles Lyell, a famous English geologist of the nineteenth century, visited New Madrid in the late 1840s and reported that the Indians of the Mississippi Valley had a legend about the great earthquake that had devastated the area. In 1811, the Shawnee chief Tecumseh was recruiting Indians from several tribes in the Mississippi Valley to try to prevent white settlers from moving into Indian lands. He traveled extensively but had very little success. Finally, in disgust, he said that when he reached Detroit he would stamp his foot and cause their houses to fall down. Some of the Indians believed he had been sent by the Great Spirit, and they dreaded his arrival in Detroit. Finally, the morning came when they thought he would have completed his journey. A great rumbling was heard, and when the noise and movement stopped, every Indian dwelling was shaken down. This was the first of the New Madrid earthquakes, and according to the legend Tecumseh had successfully predicted it.

Scientists do predict that the possibility of an earthquake on an active fault line, such as the New Madrid fault line, increases with time because stresses within the earth build up until the rocks can take no more. A sudden break in the underlying structure is inevitable.

The 1990 Earthquake Prediction

On September 26, 1990, early morning coffee drinkers across from the New Madrid County courthouse thought a large truck or a piece of heavy equipment was traveling down Main Street. Windows and dishes rattled, but most people did not realize what had caused the movement until it was over. An earthquake measuring 4.6 on the Richter scale was recorded about ten miles southwest of Cape Girardeau, fifty miles north of New Madrid. It was felt in five states and caused almost half a million dollars in property loss.

This relatively minor quake was given unusual attention because of a statement made the year before by scientist Iben Browning. In October 1989, at a business conference where he spoke to more than 500 people, Browning said that because of the positions the sun and moon would be in on December 3, 1990, there would be an enhanced chance of an earthquake on the New Madrid fault line. The last time the sun and moon had been in the same positions, he said, was in December 1811.

Browning had predicted the San Francisco earthquake on October 17, 1989, one week before it occurred. It is said that he also predicted the Mount St. Helen's eruption in 1980 and the earthquake in Mexico in 1985. The seventy-two-year-old Browning had many interests. He had a Ph.D. in biophysics, and during his long career he had worked in the fields of microbiology, mathematics, engineering, and economics. As a self-taught climatologist, he had studied the effects of climate on the earth. He was not recognized, however, by specialists in the field (seismologists and geologists) as an expert on earthquakes. These scientists believe that quakes on the New Madrid fault line can be predicted over a long span of time, but not within a span of a few days. Nevertheless, many people listened to Browning and feared that he might be right. The news media soon picked up the story. It developed in such a way that it seemed as if Browning had made an actual prediction. In fact, he had only suggested an "enhanced chance" of an earthquake.

The media reported that Browning said that smaller quakes in the New Madrid area could occur on October 9 and November 26. To some residents, the September 26 tremor was close enough to October 9 to make them believe that Browning's theory might be right. Then, in the late evening of November 8, a quake measuring 3.6 on the Richter scale occurred. These events seemed to establish Browning's ability to predict. They caused people of New Madrid to drive to Sikeston, about twenty miles north, to the nearest discount stores to buy emergency supplies. In fact, they emptied the shelves of some items. At one store, the manager announced, "If it cooks, heats, or gives off light . . . we're out of it."

New Madrid received national attention after October, when the Associated Press wire service published an account of the prediction in newspapers all over the country. For the first time, people other than those on or near the fault line sat up and took notice. In late November, and certainly by December 1,

More than twenty television stations' satellite trucks from around the country descended on New Madrid in December 1990 to cover the earthquake prediction story. Reporters "interviewed residents, tourists, and each other." (photo by Mark Sterkel, *Southeast Missourian*, December 3, 1990)

New Hamburg in Scott County was at the epicenter of one of the earthquakes in 1990, and T-shirts were sold to raise money for earthquake-preparedness supplies. Garrett Mall, left, of Kelso and Tiffany Glastetter of New Hamburg are shown in the new T-shirts. (photo by Fred Lynch, *Southeast Missourian*, October 4, 1990)

major American and foreign news networks sent reporters and photographers to New Madrid, a town whose residents admit that it usually generates little excitement. Martha Hunter, the town's librarian, said it was "quite a show." Television crews set up their equipment on Main Street and in some businesses. Many townspeople stood on street corners to watch and sometimes laugh as nationally known newspeople tried to make a story out of the reactions of residents to the prediction. They reported everything that could possibly be considered news. Attorney Lynn Bock closed his office on Monday, December 3, the day the quake was to occur. A sign in his window announced that he could not work "because the circus is coming to town."

William Clark, then owner of Tom's Grill, a five-table diner on Main Street, took his grandson's advice and hurriedly put up a sign advertising "Quake Burgers." They sold to standing-room-only crowds on December 2 and 3. Clark also had telephone interviews with reporters from all over the country; he charged a Peoria, Illinois, radio station $200 to broadcast from his diner. He was also pictured on the front page of *USA Today* on November 28, 1990. Clark's "Quake Burger" sign remains, and the burgers are still served on request.

Schools in southeast Missouri were closed on Monday, December 3, freeing some 40,000 students from class work. In White Bluff, Tennessee, the Christmas parade planned for December 3 was canceled. Meetings and conferences scheduled in St. Louis for that weekend were canceled. Towns along the fault line stepped up their earthquake preparation. In New Madrid itself, the 3,300 residents for the most part considered the "circus" created by the prediction a media event, one that was not always showing them fairly. One reporter called from Los Angeles and said to William Clark, "I hear there are a bunch of morons who thought there was goin' to be an earthquake." Clark angrily replied, "Let's get this straight. We're not morons, and we're not afraid of earthquakes. You reporters are the ones who created this."

Tom's Grill, home of the "Quake Burger." (photo by the author)

I agree with Clark. In the spring of 1994 and again in May 1995, when I visited New Madrid, there was no sign that people gave much heed to the possibility of an impending earthquake. Closing the schools December 3, 1990, was a precaution, not an act caused by fear or stupidity. Experts warn that the casualty rate is greatly increased in disasters that strike during the day, when large numbers of people are gathered in public buildings. Some estimate that injuries and deaths would be counted in the thousands if a quake occurred during normal business or school hours. Injuries and deaths might still occur if a quake occurred during night or early morning hours, but the number would be greatly reduced because people are scattered over a larger area. While there was some panic reported by the media, it came from outlying towns. Within New Madrid at the time, there was both acceptance and amusement at the furor caused by outside television, radio, and newspaper people.

Clement Cravens, writing in the *New Madrid Weekly Record* on November 30, 1990, covered the hoopla that had made New Madrid the center of national attention for the latter part of the year. "This weekend," he said, we "get to find out if Iben Browning is a quack or on track." At first, Cravens said, people were pretty excited to be the subject of so much news. Some of them liked being interviewed on television and the radio, or quoted in newspapers. But the time came when there were no more new questions, and the media, Cravens said, were about as welcome as ants at a picnic. Cravens also noted that if the prediction came true, this would be the best-covered disaster in history. He, like other locals, hoped the prediction would not come true.

For the most part, people of the Midwest took the events in stride. Stewart and Knox write that people living anywhere in the Midwest are subject to possible injury and property damage from activity on the New Madrid fault line. News reporter Burton Cole of Decatur, Illinois, 100 miles northeast of St. Louis, wrote about a seminar on earthquake preparedness held at the Rock Springs Center for Environmental Discovery at Decatur just days before the predicted quake. The seminar was attended by only nine people plus a news reporter. Among those at the seminar, several chose not to disclose their names because they were afraid they might be laughed at by family and friends.

CHAPTER 6

Preparing for an Earthquake

"The question is not whether earthquakes will happen again in the region; clearly, they will."

— James Penick Jr., *The New Madrid Earthquakes of 1811–1812*

One of the duties of the Federal Emergency Management Agency (FEMA), created in 1979, is to deal with the problem of earthquakes in the United States. The federal government was the first to show concern about earthquakes in the Mississippi Valley. FEMA has held a series of workshops and hearings since the early 1980s to share knowledge and to make the public aware of the potential risks of and possible defenses against earthquakes.

In 1981, the government created the Central United States Earthquake Consortium (CUSEC) to shift the responsibility and care from a national to a regional office. CUSEC received funding through FEMA and distributed it to the seven state governments most likely to be affected by earthquakes in the Midwest. The purpose of this funding is to enable states to educate people so that risks can be reduced. CUSEC established earthquake advisory boards to help states work together. That way, when quakes strike, they can be dealt with on a multistate level, as well as within local areas. This cooperation gives local governments the ability to call on emergency crews in nearby cities and states if their own emergency systems are put out of order by a disaster. For example, the Southern Illinois University School of Medicine in Springfield has planned for medical rescue efforts in the event of an earthquake in the area. Except for Veterans Administration hospitals, there are no earthquake-resistant hospitals in the Mississippi Valley area.

Some cities and counties are working to improve their building codes. In New Madrid, for example, the old public school within the city is boarded up, and a new, safer school has been built outside of town. St. Louis and St. Louis County are cooperating to see that uniform building codes are enforced on new structures. The cost of reinforcing every existing building is prohibitive, but communities can see to it that at least hospitals, schools, high rises, and nursing homes are protected against earthquakes. Carbondale, Illinois, has been working to improve citizen earthquake awareness since the early 1970s. The city also has a strict building code and a trained inspection officer to enforce the code. Most cities and counties are not so well prepared as St. Louis and Carbondale, however. Writer William Atkinson fears that most places will be in the same situation following a major earthquake that New Madrid was in when the earthquakes of 1811–1812 hit. In addition to the structural damage that New Madrians suffered then, the gas, water, electric power, roads, and telecommunications that people depend on today would probably be useless following a massive earthquake.

There was an important result of the attention given to the area by the media after Iben Browning's comments. People became more aware of the damage that quakes can do in the central United States. Another result is that people have been persuaded that preparations made beforehand can sizably reduce the dangers resulting from a quake.

In 1990, the Eighty-fifth Missouri General Assembly passed Senate Bill 539, a law that requires that within the forty-seven Missouri counties at risk for earthquake damage all public buildings be built to withstand earthquakes. The law further requires that every school within those counties plan emergency earthquake procedures and that earthquake drills be held twice each year. David Stewart, then director of the Center for Earthquake Studies at Southeast Missouri State University, praised the action of the lawmakers; he believes that being prepared will make a significant difference in survival following a disaster. He also points out that it is crucial that the soil that public buildings are located on be stable. Clay soils, which can turn to liquid in an earthquake, should be bypassed in favor of more stable ground. St. Louis, for example, is in less danger of serious earthquake damage than Memphis because it is built on a solid rock foundation.

The center has trained people who can now teach others about earthquake risks and how to avoid them. In New Madrid, in September 1990, Stewart addressed a standing-room-only

Center for Earthquake Studies, Cape Girardeau. In 1990, the center had seven full-time staff members and occupied the entire building. By 1995 the staff had been reduced to one, and space had been reduced to half of the building. (photo by the author)

crowd at the town's Dixie Theater when he spoke about what to do before, during, and after an earthquake.

Home Preparedness

No home will survive a massive earthquake that is centered right underneath it, but that is not likely to happen to one's home. A sensible approach to protecting property and maintaining safety for those within the areas of VIII and higher on the CUSEC Intensity Map is to follow the guidelines set out by CUSEC. The following precautions should be taken:

- Frame houses should have the corners braced and basement walls reinforced.
- Chimneys should be no taller than necessary, with no loose bricks.
- Water heaters should be firmly attached to walls with metal straps to prevent their breaking away from water pipes and gas or electric lines.
- Large, heavy objects should be kept at low levels to prevent them from falling and injuring people.
- Tall, heavy furniture should be bolted to walls to prevent it from falling forward and injuring people.
- It may be best to replace heavy lighting fixtures to prevent injury.
- In the garden, weak trees should be cut down; otherwise, they can break power lines and fall on people or houses.

Precautions to be taken if an earthquake seems imminent, as in the December 1990 scare, include

- Electricity and gas should be turned off. Usually communities have automatic gas cutoffs in the event of emergencies. The gas company, for example, does not recommend that residents turn off the gas supply at their own meters.
- Water may need to be shut off at the major valve entering the home. In the event of an emergency requiring water shutoff

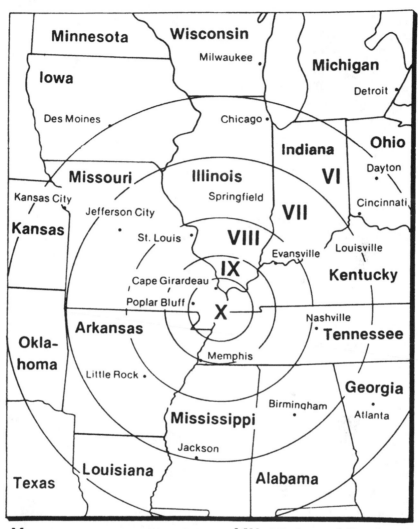

X Widespread destruction **VII** Slight architectural
IX Structural damage   damage
VIII Weak structures damaged, **VI** Furniture moves,
 chimneys fall   trees sway

This map shows the intensities that a major earthquake on the New Madrid fault would have in different parts of the region. Damage would be most severe at the epicenter, the area directly above the earth's surface at the place of origin of an earthquake, marked by X on the map. (*Columbia Missourian,* December 18, 1985)

by the community, people should have enough clean water stored in their water heaters for several days of emergency use *if* their own meters have been shut off from the main supply before contaminated water could get into them.
• Doors to cabinets should be latched to prevent them from opening and allowing the contents to fall out.
• Families should develop a plan of action to take during a quake and rehearse the plan.
• Safe spots should be noted for each room in the home, and each family member should know where those spots are.

William Atkinson suggests that people take a tour of their home and grounds and imagine a fairy-tale giant lifting everything and shaking it. What would be damaged? How dangerous could such a shaking be to the family? How can such damage be prevented?

CUSEC has outlined the steps one should take when an earthquake occurs. The outline points out that there will be no warning. It states that shaking usually lasts only twenty to sixty seconds, but according to several eyewitness reports on the quakes of 1811–1812, the more severe ones lasted two to four minutes. A few eyewitness reports said that one or two lasted up to ten minutes. Most injuries happen early in the quake and are the result of falling debris. If you are indoors,

• Stay indoors; falling power lines and trees can be dangerous outdoors.
• Take cover under a desk or strong table by an inside wall. An inside doorway can be protection, but sometimes doors slam during quakes.
• Stay away from windows and outside doors and walls.
• Do not use telephones or elevators.
• Do not strike a match until gas lines are checked.
• Prepare for aftershocks, which can be as strong as, or stronger than, the first quake.
• Put on sturdy shoes before moving after tremors stop. There is apt to be broken glass following a quake.

If you are outdoors,

- Stay there, but move away from buildings and utility lines. Sit in an open area with your head down and protected by your arms.
- If you are driving, pull to the side of the road and stop. Stay in the car.
- Do not stop the car on a bridge or under an overpass.

Checklist for Survival

William Atkinson suggests that survival materials should be stored in a place where they will be available following a severe earthquake. Their safe storage can make a family independent of community resources for a week. The following suggested items are based on Atkinson's list:

- Water: seven gallons per person, enough for one week. It needs to be replaced regularly, probably every thirty days, but water stored in the freezer needs to be changed only yearly.
- Bleach to purify water.
- Food: canned food that includes meats, vegetables, fruits, and juices. Food should be replaced twice annually; as new items are purchased, they can be dated as they replace older items on the shelf.
- One flashlight, with spare batteries, for each adult.
- Candles and matches.
- First aid equipment, including a first aid book, soap, alcohol, hydrogen peroxide, aspirin, small bandages, sanitary napkins, scissors, knife, and any special medications regularly used by a member of the family.
- Handsaw, crescent wrench, hammer and nails, pry bar, and 100 feet of rope.
- Warm clothing with changes, including sturdy shoes. Blankets, sleeping bags.
- Paper plates, can opener, paper towels, plastic knives, forks, and spoons.

First aid supplies, batteries, bottled water, and canned goods sold out quickly after a September 1990 earthquake measuring 4.6 on the Richter scale. Cape Girardeau Wal-Mart employee Lori Pruitt arranges first aid supplies on the almost-empty shelves. (*Southeast Missourian* photo, September 27, 1990)

- Toilet tissue, trash bags, food for pets, extra eyeglasses, reading and writing materials, toothpaste, deodorant, shampoo.

CUSEC covers the survival list in more detail in brochures that are available from the Center for Earthquake Studies, One University Plaza, Cape Girardeau, MO 63701.

Paying attention to these suggestions will help us protect ourselves, our families, and our homes and businesses in an emergency. Electric cooperatives in the New Madrid area are prepared for an emergency as best they can be, but they still expect that area customers may be without electric power for days, perhaps weeks, in the event of an earthquake. They are training people in the area and are connected to a statewide plan that will allow them to call the state headquarters in Jefferson City to make arrangements for crews from other electric cooperatives from unaffected parts of the state to be sent to help.

We cannot avoid earthquakes, but through careful preparation, we can lessen to a substantial degree the panic that people feel and reduce the property damage and loss of life that occur.

CHAPTER 7

Toward the Twentieth Century

"The citizens did not lose faith in the final prosperity of their town and they did not abandon it."

— Robert Sidney Douglass, *History of Southeast Missouri*

In spite of the dangers that the Mississippi River posed when it overflowed its bounds and changed its course, and in spite of the threat of future earthquakes, people did not stay away long from the river cities of southeast Missouri. From 1820 to 1830, the population in the region increased steadily, especially along the Mississippi River. The new people moving in were mostly old stock Americans or European immigrants. New Madrid County, though it was much smaller after its final boundaries were drawn, had twice the number of people in 1850 that it had in 1820.

Along the river, the lands were so fertile, trade and transportation so good, that new settlers saw a bright future for themselves and their families. Most of the new buildings were constructed of lumber, rather than logs, because people believed that frame buildings would withstand quakes better than log buildings. In 1822 the county seat moved back to New Madrid following a ten-year period of being inland. It has remained in New Madrid ever since. The courthouse was rebuilt three times—each time of frame—during the nineteenth century because of flooding.

This sketch of the eastern part of New Madrid in 1826, by Charles A. LeSueur, was copied by Charles Peterson from the original in the Museum of Natural History in Le Havre, France. (State Historical Society of Missouri, Columbia)

Then, in 1905, the building was destroyed by fire. The current courthouse of brick and stone was built in 1915 and occupies a prominent place on Main Street.

By 1837 New Madrid had a population of 450. According to a report organized by Hunter Miller for the New Madrid County Teachers Association in 1948, St. Joseph's Parochial school had been established in 1832, as the "Young Ladies Academy." There was also a Catholic church and a nunnery housing the school's teachers, the Sisters of Loretta of Bethlehem. The school was closed five years later; because of fevers and illnesses the nuns were recalled. The school was reopened in 1916 and has remained in existence since then. The first public schools were opened in about 1870.

In the early nineteenth century, Samuel Dorsey had a successful medical practice in the town. Another physician, H. M.

This painting, by Henry Lewis, shows New Madrid as it looked in about 1848. The painting was printed in *Das Illustrirte Mississippithal* or *The Illustrated Mississippi Valley.* (State Historical Society of Missouri, Columbia)

Chisholm, settled in New Madrid, but he chose to farm rather than practice medicine during his years there.

As the Civil War began, most southeast Missourians wanted to save the Union, but when secession occurred, the majority sided with the South. The Mississippi River became very important to the transportation of people and arms during the war, and the Union needed control of the river for that reason. Island 10, south of New Madrid about ten miles by land, held a garrison of 7,000 heavily armed Confederate soldiers who controlled river traffic from that point south. Historian John Fiske writes a compelling description of how the Union Army, headed by General John Pope, gained control of the island and, ultimately, the river. In the spring of 1862, with 20,000 men, he established a base at Point Pleasant, Missouri, twelve miles south of New Madrid, cutting off supplies to the town from the south. The

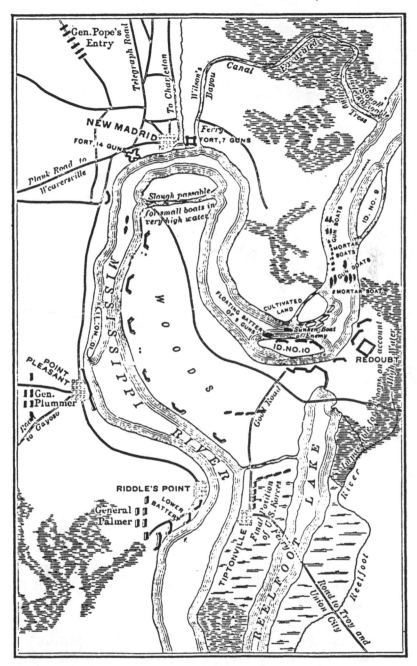

Map showing the Confederate fortifications on the Mississippi River at Island 10 and New Madrid. (State Historical Society of Missouri)

Union troops then dug a canal north of island 9 to permit Union boats access from the north. The next step was to secure island 10 and its garrison of Confederate soldiers.

The move was so dangerous that no one was assigned to take it on, but Commander Henry Walke volunteered to run by the island in the *Carondelet,* a gunboat, under cover of darkness. The boat was covered with wood planks and bales of hay to protect it from enemy fire. Walke steered the boat so close to the island that the Confederate cannon fire went harmlessly overhead. The Union Army thus gained island 10 and control of the Mississippi River. The Tiptonville Road, the only escape route from island 10, was secured by the Union forces, and the Confederates surrendered to them. New Madrid was taken over by the Union. A large part of the town was destroyed during the siege.

In 1852 there were only five miles of railroad in all of Missouri. In 1857 the Ohio and Mississippi Railroad connected St. Louis to the East. By 1899 the St. Louis Southwestern Railroad made it to New Madrid on a branch that ran from Lilbourn to New Madrid. Following that, a new railroad line from New Madrid to Marston was completed by the Frisco Railroad. The first newspaper in New Madrid, the *Gazette,* was published from 1846 to 1854. It then changed ownership and was published as the *Times* until the Civil War. The *New Madrid Weekly Record* was established in 1866 and is still in operation. New Madrid was incorporated as a city, second class, in 1878, with John Brownell as mayor.

The Catholic Church assigned a pastor to New Madrid in 1867, and its Church of the Immaculate Conception was dedicated in 1869. The Methodists are the oldest Protestant group in New Madrid; they established a congregation there in 1810 and built their first church in 1847. The Presbyterians came in 1856 and built their first church in 1875.

At the beginning of the twentieth century, New Madrid had railway service and a public school system. The town also boasted two hotels, two sawmills, one flour mill, two cotton

Island 10 with steamboat. (State Historical Society of Missouri, Columbia) gins, and about thirty stores where people could buy a large assortment of merchandise. There was also a gristmill, some woodworking plants, and electric and waterworks plants. New Madrid remained an important river city, welcoming trade from the river and meeting the needs of river travelers while maintaining itself as a healthy, thriving town that continued to grow in population and serve the farmers who lived in and near the city.

CHAPTER 8

New Madrid Today

"Living on the New Madrid fault line, / You've gotta live it day by day."

— Lou Hobbs, song lyrics to "Living on the New Madrid Fault Line"

When Sikeston, Missouri, twenty miles north of New Madrid, became the site of a new Wal-Mart store twenty or more years ago, it changed the pace in both towns. Sikeston has attracted other stores and now boasts a discount mall; it became a thriving community that attracts business and visitors. New Madrid's shops closed, one by one, so that only small convenience markets adjacent to filling stations remain. One woman who sews for her family told me that she can no longer buy even a spool of thread in town.

Librarian Martha Hunter remembers going downtown as a girl on Saturday afternoons when the town was abuzz with activity. "We'd drive downtown Saturday morning and park the car on Main Street, walk back home, and then have the car ready so we could sit in it in late afternoon and watch the passing people." Now there are occasionally a few visitors and some activity at the courthouse, but there is no bowling alley, no theater, no drugstore soda fountain, no place for young people to gather. Hunter now knows why her father advised her to "shop at home."

This view from the levee shows New Madrid as it looks today. *Missouri: A Guide to the "Show-Me" State* observes that New Madrid's main streets are at right angles to the river. "Unconsciously the town expresses the interest of its citizens, who keep one eye on the Mississippi and one eye on the hills." The New Madrid Museum is in the building to the right in the foreground. (photo by the author)

There are still two restaurants downtown. Tom's Grill, across from the courthouse, was my choice for breakfast on a recent visit. A country plateful of sausage and eggs with juice, toast, and coffee were perfectly prepared and served. There was the regular slamming of two wood-framed screen doors at Tom's as men came and went that morning. My friend and I and the waitress were the only women there at 9 A.M. I was lulled by the sound of southern voices and felt a closeness to my ancestors as the melodic accents filled the room. Some of the men were eating breakfast; most were just drinking coffee while they shared stories and caught up on local affairs. Most of the men appeared to be retired farmers, but later we saw two of them working on the levee.

The River Bend Cafe, across from the Chamber of Commerce office, was built by Jack Hailey and two friends two years ago. It opens near 11 A.M., in time for lunch. Pork chops more than an inch thick were the entree on the Wednesday we were there. At the River Bend, Hailey keeps serving the day's special until he runs out; you would not want to delay going much past 1 P.M. if you were counting on the special. Hailey also serves dinner, with emphasis on fish and seafood.

The New Madrid Historical Museum, located near the levee, houses artifacts of the town's history. On one wall is a splendid silk and velvet friendship quilt with 900 signatures of nine-teenth-century New Madrid residents. It was made in 1886 by St. Ann's Catholic Church Sodality as a fund-raiser. There are glass cases holding dolls, dental tools, and other things one might expect to see in a local museum. On the walls are photographs and numerous notices. It was on one of these notices that I learned that Robert G. Watson, born in Scotland, came to New Madrid in 1804 and was a licensed merchant in the town until his death in 1855. This and other evidence shows that New Madrid was a market town at the time of the earthquakes and that, contrary to Ben Chartier's story reported earlier, there were stores in New Madrid in 1811.

A room in the museum housing the gift shop is devoted to dis-plays and equipment related to earthquakes. New Madrid High School graduates of 1940 donated a seismograph to the mu-seum. It is prominently placed in the room and runs constantly, collecting seismic activity from all over the world and printing the results on paper tapes. The museum director showed me where earlier tapes are stored in the bottom drawer of a cabinet; they report activity in Egypt and Japan, among other places. An audiovisual program in a permanent display tells about earth-quakes as they affect the New Madrid fault line. A "cuenometer" sits in a corner near a window; it is an earthquake prediction experiment. Earthquake expert Stewart has one in his home.

A cuenometer is meant to detect extremely low frequency sounds. Prior to earthquakes, the earth may make low frequency noises as it gets ready to snap. Keith Morin, an electronics technician and inventor, was successful in the late 1980s in predicting a quake in San Francisco using information he read from a cuenometer. He was able to predict the time (off by only eight hours), place, and magnitude (within 0.2 on the Richter scale) of the quake; so the method has worked at least once. If such low frequency noises do occur, they could be helpful in predicting earthquakes here. They could also explain the strange behavior of animals prior to quakes.

Much of the swampy land around New Madrid caused by the earthquake has been reclaimed by an extensive drainage system. Rich farmland surrounds the town, but scars remain. Most of the scars are sand boils that were formed during the quake. Sand boils are patches of sand that boil gently to the surface during earthquakes and leave cone-shaped pits of sand. At the time of the quakes, these pits were filled with quicksand. Now the pits are filled with sand, ten or more feet deep. The largest sand boil in the New Madrid area is about 500 feet in diameter. Other circular sand boil scars also remain. Most of the scars or boils are considerably smaller than 500 feet and are surrounded by fields, but they are easily visible from the air. Nothing will grow on these boils.

The town's public high school was closed and replaced in the 1980s by a new one less likely to succumb to earthquakes. The Catholic school is not subject to new earthquake-proofing codes, but the parish decided several years ago to meet the requirements anyway. Strong diagonal braces are visible in the classrooms, and metal plates are hidden in the ceilings for protection from falling debris. The teachers and children of the Immaculate Conception School have T-shirts that read "I. C. School, Retrofitted for Rock n' Roll." At the museum in New Madrid, T-shirts, sweatshirts, and book bags claim "It's Our Fault."

Who thought up those slogans? Who knows? The point is that the humor and irony are appreciated and enjoyed by the folk of New Madrid. Humor and intelligence were obvious to me as

This view of New Madrid from the air, looking east, was taken in April 1991. The white spots on the ground are the sand boils that were created during the earthquakes of 1811–1812. (David Stewart and Ray Knox, slide no. 12 from *The Earthquake that Never Went Away*, 1993)

I talked with people in the courthouse, the cafes, the Chamber of Commerce office, the newspaper office, and the library.

I strolled along the embankment separating the town from the mighty Mississippi and walked out on the observation platform built in 1989. From that vantage point, I could see partially submerged trees, the river that is otherwise hidden from the town, and the Kentucky shore. The attraction of the river was as evident to me then as it was to my mother in the 1920s. She played on its banks and got its mud between her toes. Like me, she listened to its lull, sometimes its roar, and was lured by its mystery and the invitation it offered to lands far away, indeed to all of the world.

In 1990, the population of New Madrid was 3,350; in New Madrid County, the population was 21,000. The Catholic church remains strong in New Madrid, as does the Methodist church.

Lou Hobbs of Cape
Girardeau, a country
and western entertainer,
performed his song
about life on the
New Madrid fault line
for an NBC team in
New Madrid during
the December 1990
media coverage of the
earthquake prediction.
(photo by David Hente,
Southeast Missourian,
December 3, 1990)

There are now three Baptist churches, one Jehovah's Witness
hall, and a Pentecostal church. The advertisers appearing on
New Madrid television sets now come more often from television stations in Tennessee, Illinois, or Kentucky than from
stations in Missouri. People may have to go out of town to buy
thread, groceries, and other supplies, but they return to the quiet
and dignity of their town.

The people of New Madrid are serene about any impending
threat of earthquake. They go about their daily chores with little
or no concern for what might be taking place under them. New
Madrians know the fault is there, they even acknowledge it as
their own, but they are not going to panic or stop daily activity
because of it. As Lou Hobbs says in his song about the area's people and their life on the fault line, they "gotta live it day by day."

Mercalli Intensity Scale

The Mercalli scale for measuring the intensity of earthquakes was developed in 1902 by an Italian priest and geologist, Giuseppe Mercalli. It was modified in 1931 to include descriptions of damage for modern structures. The Mercalli scale is a method of measuring, using personal judgment, the intensity of ground movement and putting it into categories on a scale of I to XII. Thus, at its epicenter a quake may measure XI on the Mercalli scale, but as the movement spreads away from the center, the intensity of movement lessens until it is barely felt, and the Mercalli numbers assigned to the intensity levels decrease.

Each level of intensity on the Mercalli scale is described below. As the numbers increase on the Mercalli scale, the damage for that category includes that listed for that number plus that of all the numbers before it.

I

Movement is not felt except in unusual circumstances. Sometimes animals seem uneasy.

II

Some movement is felt indoors by a few people, especially on upper floors. Light hanging objects may swing.

III

A tremor can be felt indoors, as if a heavy truck had passed on the street, but most people do not recognize the movement as an earthquake. It may be noticeable on upper floors of buildings.

IV

The tremor is felt indoors by many, outdoors by some. It rattles dishes, and people can see movement of liquids in open containers, such as toilets.

V

Motion is felt indoors by most, outdoors by many. It awakens people from sleep, overturns small objects, and may stop pendulum clocks. Trees shake; there is some broken glass and cracked plaster.

VI

Movement is felt by everyone, indoors and out. Liquids are set in strong motion, and trees shake. Cracked plaster damages some buildings, and fine cracks may appear in chimneys. X-shaped cracks in brick walls covered in stucco are typical. Poorly built or older buildings may be heavily damaged.

VII

This temblor frightens everyone. Brick walls may collapse, and some people find it difficult to stand. Trees are shaken strongly, and waves appear on open water. Damage to poorly built buildings is considerable. Chimneys may be cracked, windows broken, and heavy furniture overturned.

VIII

Tremor causes general fright approaching panic and can be felt by persons driving automobiles. Trees and branches are broken. Sand and mud are spurted in small amounts from the earth. Damage from partial collapse of sturdy buildings occurs. Solid stone walls will be cracked or broken.

IX

Movement causes general panic. Some frame houses built to withstand earthquakes are thrown out of plumb. Masonry buildings will be damaged as well. Some underground pipes will be broken, and there is serious threat to reservoirs.

X

Motion cracks the ground. Landslides occur from river banks and steep coasts. The level of water in wells is changed; water is thrown up on the banks of rivers and lakes. There are dangerous cracks in brick walls; most masonry and frame structures are destroyed. Serious damage to dams and embankments occurs, as do open cracks in cement and asphalt roads.

XI

Quake causes great damage to frame buildings and to most masonry structures as well. Well-built bridges are destroyed, and pipelines buried in the ground are not usable. Broad fissures appear in the ground, and water mixed with sand and mud is spurted from the ground in large amounts.

XII

At this intensity, damage is total. Almost every human-made structure is damaged or destroyed. Landslides, rock falls, and falling of riverbanks occur. Land may be seen to wave. All water bodies, underground and surface, are disturbed and changed.

Note: The sources for this explanation of the scale are Otto W. Nuttli, *The Effects of Earthquakes in the Central United States*, 2nd ed. (Cape Girardeau, Mo.: Center for Earthquake Studies, 1990), pages 2–3; and William Atkinson, *The Next New Madrid Earthquake: A Survival Guide for the Midwest* (Carbondale: Southern Illinois University Press, 1989), pages 157–61.

Richter Magnitude Scale

The Mercalli scale may be used to describe an earthquake either at its epicenter or at any point in the area into which the effects of the earthquake extend. The Richter scale, devised in 1935 by American seismologist Charles F. Richter, measures the intensity of the quake at its epicenter. Both the Mercalli and the Richter scales measure in numbers, with the greatest damage being assigned the highest number. The Richter measurement is made by instruments called seismometers, which are located at recording stations all over the world.

David Stewart and Ray Knox are contemporary scientists who have studied and written extensively about the New Madrid Seismic Zone. They point out that every added 1.0 unit on the Richter scale represents thirty-two times the difference in energy released by a quake. Thus, a 6.0 quake on the Richter scale is thirty-two times stronger than one measuring 5.0. Every 0.2 increase in the scale doubles the intensity of the quake. Thus, a 5.2 quake releases twice the energy as does one measuring 5.0.

Stewart also points out that the Richter scale is in a constantly developing state. The original scale as it was devised by Richter is rarely used by anyone today. In his book *Damages and Losses from Future New Madrid Earthquakes,* Stewart points out the discrepancies that occur in measuring magnitudes. There are five different ways to calculate magnitude from available instruments, and scientists generally report to the media the highest number recorded. Scientists have agreed on adjectives to define the way we can consider the numbers on the Richter scale.

Adjectives to Describe Richter Numbers

Great	8.0 or larger
Major	7.0 – 7.9
Strong	6.0 – 6.9
Moderate	5.0 – 5.9
Light	4.0 – 4.9
Minor	3.0 – 3.9
Very Minor	2.9 or less

It may be important to point out again here that the Richter measurements are not always consistent. Machines may vary by 0.2 of a point on the Richter scale, and this fact takes on extra significance when we recognize that an increase of 0.2 in the scale doubles the intensity of the quake.

Comparison of Earthquake Magnitude and Intensity

Richter Magnitude	*Mercalli Intensity*
8.0–8.9	XI–XII
7.0–7.9	IX–X
6.0–6.9	VII–VIII
5.0–5.9	VI–VII
4.0–4.9	IV–V
3.0–3.9	II–III
Below 3.0	I

Note: Though there is no upper limit to the Richter magnitude scale, 8.9 is the largest number ever reported.

Note: The latter chart is adapted from one used by William Atkinson in *The Next New Madrid Earthquake: A Survival Guide for the Midwest* (Carbondale: Southern Illinois University Press, 1989), page 37.

For More Reading

The Amazing Voyage of the New Orleans, by Judith St. George (New York: G. P. Putnam's Sons, 1980), is for children, ages four to eight, and is illustrated by Glen Rounds with pencil sketches. It tells about the 2,000-mile voyage of the *New Orleans,* the first steamboat in western waters (in 1811) and its experience in the New Madrid earthquake.

Audubon and His Journals, by John James Audubon (New York: Scribner's, 1897; reprint, Dover, 1960), includes Audubon's reaction to one of the quakes he felt while riding his horse in Kentucky. Audubon also discussed what life was like for new settlers west of the Mississippi River in the early nineteenth century.

Damages and Losses from Future New Madrid Earthquakes, by David Stewart (Cape Girardeau, Mo.: Center for Earthquake Studies, 2nd printing, 1992), covers in detail the New Madrid fault, the possibility of another earthquake such as the quakes of 1811–1812, and the steps to be taken to avoid disaster. It includes important facts regarding the Richter scale from the point of view of a specialist in the field. Definitions of terms are clearly written. Illustrated with charts and maps.

Earthquake: The Story of Alaska's Good Friday Disaster, by Eloise Engle (New York: John Day, 1966), discusses other earthquakes of importance, as well as the Alaska disaster in 1964 and the New Madrid earthquake.

The Earthquake America Forgot: 2000 Temblors in Five Months . . . And It Will Happen Again!, by David Stewart and Ray Knox (Marble Hill, Mo.: Gutenberg-Richter Publications, 1995), is a comprehensive look at the New Madrid earthquake and how it affected people and the land. The authors include predictions for future quakes along the New Madrid Seismic Zone; their scientific data is liberally sprinkled with folksy stories, humor, and many little-known facts.

"The Earthquake Guide for Home and Office" is a brochure prepared by the Center for Earthquake Studies at Southeast Missouri State University that gives helpful hints about how to prepare for and survive a coming earthquake. Available from the Center for Earthquake Studies, Southeast Missouri State University, One University Plaza, Cape Girardeau, MO 63701.

The Earthquake of 1811, by Timothy Dudley (Washington, D.C.: James B. Stedman, 1859), is a recounting of the events of the New Madrid earthquake told to Dudley fifty years after it occurred.

"The Earthquake of 1811 and Its Influence on Evangelistic Methods in Churches of the Old South," by Walter Brownlow Posey (*Tennessee Historical Magazine*, January 1931, pp. 109–11), gives figures on church membership and recounts stories of preachers who gloried in the discomfort of "sinners."

The Earthquake that Never Went Away: The Shaking Stopped in 1812, but the Impact Goes On, by David Stewart and Ray Knox (Marble Hill, Mo.: Gutenberg-Richter Publications, 1993), combines scientific knowledge with folksy information to create an appealing story about how and why earthquakes happen in the Mississippi Valley. The writers have produced a set of over 100 slides to accompany this text so that people can present programs about Mississippi Valley earthquakes. Illustrated with black-and-white photographs.

Earthquakes, by Nicholas Hunter Heck (Princeton, N.J.: Princeton University Press, 1936), refers to the New Madrid quakes in several places, pointing out the changes in land, the creation of Reelfoot Lake, and the devastation over large areas.

The Effects of Earthquakes in the Central United States, 2nd ed., by Otto W. Nuttli (Cape Girardeau, Mo.: Center for Earthquake Studies, 1990), was revised with a foreword and appendices by David Stewart, then director of the Center. The revised publication includes black-and-white photographs of damage caused by earthquakes, as well as charts and predictions of future quakes in the Midwest.

Fury in the Earth: A Novel of the New Madrid Earthquake, by Henry Harrison Kroll (Indianapolis: Bobbs-Merrill, 1945), is a story about the earthquake that includes historical persons as characters. For example, Eliza Bryan is a major character in this novel as a schoolteacher. Kroll dwells on action and includes some gore, but he also includes references to things such as pokeberry ink and a quill pen that illustrate the way people may have lived in New Madrid at that time.

"Future Shock," by Bob Schwaller (*Missouri Life*, July–August 1980, pp. 19–21), tells about the earthquakes of 1811–1812 and the plans made to protect people and property when the next one hits.

The Genesis of Missouri: From Wilderness Outpost to Statehood, by William E. Foley (Columbia: University of Missouri Press, 1989), tells about the early settling of New Madrid as well as earlier exploration of the area by the Spanish and the French.

George Morgan, Colony Builder, by Max Savelle (New York: Columbia University Press, 1932), is a biography of the man who had a vision for New Madrid as a major city in the Spanish territory of the 1790s.

Goodspeed's History of Southeast Missouri (Chicago: Goodspeed Publishing, 1888) includes some reference to the earthquakes of 1811–1812 and a listing of the settlements in Missouri and their settlement dates prior to 1811.

Great Earthquakes, by Charles Davison (London: Thomas Murley, 1936), includes a discussion of the quakes of New Madrid in 1811–1812.

The Great Shaking, by Jo Carson (New York: Orchard, 1994), is a picture book for young children, aged two to eight, illustrated in full color by Robert Andrew Parker. Set at the time and in the place of the earthquakes of 1811–1812, the story tells about a bear awaking from his hibernation early when Mother Earth seemed to him to be rising from her sleep.

History of a Cosmopolite, by Lorenzo Dow (Cincinnati: A. S. Robertson, 1850), includes the complete letter Lorenzo Dow asked Eliza Bryan to write to him describing the earthquakes as she experienced them.

History of Southeast Missouri, by Robert Sidney Douglass (New York: Lewis, 1912; reprint, Cape Girardeau, Mo.: Ramfre Press, 1961), includes a chapter on the New Madrid earthquake and gives a good overview of the people who were there, the damage done, and the effects on the people and the land.

"I Was There!" In the New Madrid Earthquakes of 1811–12 (Eyewitness Accounts by Survivors of the Worst Earthquake in American History), compiled and edited by David R. Logsdon (Nashville, Tenn.: Kettle Mills Press, 1990), is made up of recollections of people who witnessed the quakes. Logsdon has placed the retellings in chronological order to re-create the terror felt by ordinary people.

"A Major Earthquake Zone on the Mississippi," by Arch C. Johnston (*Scientific American,* April 1982, pp. 60–68), points out that the strongest earthquakes have hit the Midwest, not California, and that the shaking continues with one small quake every two days. Illustrated with photographs, drawings, maps, and charts.

Missouri, the Heart of the Nation, 2nd ed., by William E. Parrish, Charles T. Jones Jr., and Lawrence O. Christensen (Arlington Heights, Ill.: Harlan Davidson, 1992), is a history of Missouri. It includes a map of the counties of Missouri in 1811.

Missouri: Its People and Its Progress, by Earl A. Collins and Albert F. Elsea (St. Louis: Webster Publishing, 1948), deals with the changes made in Missouri, most of them prior to statehood in 1821.

Missouri: Midland State, rev. ed., by Earl A. Collins and Felix Eugene Snider (Cape Girardeau, Mo.: Ramfre Press, 1961), lists important dates leading to statehood and points out that the state's greatest growth in population occurred in 1810–1820, when Missouri grew from 19,783 to 66,586 people, a growth of over 300 percent in ten years. The authors also note that in 1799 New Madrid was the gateway for all trade between the Allegheny Mountains and the Gulf of Mexico by way of the Mississippi River.

The New Madrid Earthquake, by Myron L. Fuller (Washington: Government Printing Office, 1912, Bulletin 12; reprint, Cape Giradeau, Mo.: Ramfre Press, 1966), is an early look at the earthquake by a scientist. This comprehensive text is illustrated with charts, maps, and black-and-white photographs.

The New Madrid Earthquakes, Revised Edition, by James Penick Jr. (Columbia: University of Missouri Press, 1981), is a collection of information that was printed in newspapers and journals of the early nineteenth century that gives a clear, comprehensive look at the quakes. Penick cites as sources those most affected, male and female residents, unschooled and educated, to give a vivid picture of the quakes and make predictions about the future. Illustrated with maps and drawings.

The Next New Madrid Earthquake: A Survival Guide for the Midwest, by William Atkinson (Carbondale: Southern Illinois University Press, 1989), is a detailed account of the New Madrid quakes and includes a compelling rationale about the next quakes, as well as specific instructions on how to survive them.

"Nightmare on the Mississippi: The New Madrid Earthquakes," by Carolyn V. Platt (*Timeline,* a publication of the Ohio Historical Society, September–October 1993, pp. 18–31), contains an overview of the history of the time, as well as a clear look at the damage of the quakes. Illustrated with charts and drawings.

Recollections of the Last Ten Years, by Timothy Flint (New York: Knopf, 1932), records, within the ten years, Flint's impressions of 1819–1820, when he was in New Madrid as a Presbyterian minister. He also reports on the events eight years prior to his residence in New Madrid as he heard them from local residents.

"The Rift, the River and the Earthquake," by Arch C. Johnston (*Earth,* January 1992, pp. 34–43), describes the story of the New Madrid Seismic Zone, tells about the quakes of 1811–1812, and suggests what could happen in the future.

Some Happenings of the New Madrid Earthquake, 1811–1812, compiled by Dorothy H. Halstead, is a privately printed, undated brochure prepared for the New Madrid Historical Museum. It is available at the museum.

For More Information

Materials can be obtained from several state and federal agencies:

The Missouri State Emergency Management Agency
P.O. Box 116
Jefferson City, MO 65102
Phone: (573) 751–9571

Center for Earthquake Studies
Southeast Missouri State University
One University Plaza
Cape Girardeau, MO 63701

Central United States Earthquake Consortium
2630 East Holmes Road
Memphis, TN 38118

Gutenberg-Richter Publications
Route 1, Box 646
Marble Hill, MO 63764
Phone: 1–800–758–8629

About the Author

Norma Hayes Bagnall was born and raised in St. Louis. She has lived most of her adult life in Texas and entered Texas A&M University as a freshman in the fall of 1969, a member of the first class that openly admitted women. (Until fall 1969 the only women admitted to TAMU were wives or daughters of TAMU professors or students.) She returned to Missouri in 1981, when she became a faculty member at Missouri Western State College in St. Joseph. She is a Professor of English at the college and also Director of the Writing Project at St. Joseph. She writes monthly reviews of children's books for the St. Joseph *News-Press* and reads to children weekly at Edison Elementary School in St. Joseph, encouraging the children to write and play-act

The author with first graders at Edison Elementary School, St. Joseph. (photo by Lynn Watkins)

in response to books. She is past-president of the international Children's Literature Association and was a Fulbright exchange teacher in Wales in 1987–1988, teaching at what is now the University of Glamorgan.

Bagnall has four daughters (Ruth, Linda, Rebecca, and Amy) and one son (David). She now lives in St. Joseph, Missouri, in her Victorian home, where she does a lot of reading and some writing.